THE PROBLEM OF
JESUS

STUDY GUIDE

THE PROBLEM OF
JESUS

STUDY GUIDE — NINE SESSIONS

ANSWERING A SKEPTIC'S CHALLENGES
TO THE SCANDAL OF JESUS

MARK CLARK

WITH BETH GRAYBILL

ZONDERVAN
REFLECTIVE

ZONDERVAN REFLECTIVE

The Problem of Jesus Study Guide
Copyright © 2021 by Mark Clark

Requests for information should be addressed to:
Zondervan, 3900 *Sparks Dr. SE, Grand Rapids, Michigan 49546*

Zondervan titles may be purchased in bulk for educational, business, fundraising, or sales promotional use. For information, please email SpecialMarkets@Zondervan.com.

ISBN 978-0-310-10837-5 (softcover)

ISBN 978-0-310-10838-2 (ebook)

Published in association with the literary agency of The Fedd Agency, Post Office Box 341973, Austin, TX 78734.

Cover Design: Jenna Ritsema
Cover Photo: Public Domain
Interior Design: Denise Froehlich

Printed in the United States of America

21 22 23 24 25 26 27 28 29 30 31 32 /LSC/ 16 15 14 13 12 11 10 9 8 7 6 5 4 3 2 1

Contents

A Note from
MARK CLARK

Welcome to *The Problem of Jesus Study Guide*. This guide, including nine teaching sessions, is meant to be a companion learning experience to my book *The Problem of Jesus*. And here's why this study is so important: the life and teachings of Jesus are reality-altering events that force us to rethink and reconfigure everything about our lives—they are not just historical events we dust off and examine like artifacts in a museum. Do you know why? Because Jesus was *scandalous*. Maybe that's not the Jesus you grew up with or learned about in Sunday school. But that's the Jesus we read about in Scripture. Jesus taught eternal principles such as the Golden Rule and showed us a better way to be human, but he was also a walking controversy. He disturbed peace, challenged the status quo, and made life less safe for the people around him. Over and over again, the Bible tells us exactly how Jesus disrupted life, offended people, and shocked his loved ones. He was scandalous and often stirred the pot. This was the problem of Jesus.

This study examines why Jesus was such a scandal in the ancient world and what that scandal has to do with our lives today. Jesus confronts, challenges, and comforts us in modern society in the same way he did for first-century Jews. But there are a few twists unique to our time and culture that we will explore throughout this series—including the truth that, in the end, we actually have to pick a side and choose whether or not to follow Jesus. And yet most people in modern society would prefer to live in the uncommitted middle of staying "neutral" towards Jesus. But Jesus doesn't allow for a lukewarm agreement or a partial acceptance. That place doesn't exist with Jesus. There is no easy way around the problem of Jesus for any of us. And this creates a crisis for each of us.

That's why this study guide and the accompanying video study are designed to help you understand the crisis and decide what to do about it as we dig deeper into the problem of Jesus together. In this study, we will explore everything about Jesus: *his historical existence, his life and ministry, his parables, his claim to be God, his miracles, his death, and his resurrection*. Although you may have picked this study because it's about Jesus, in a sense, it is more about *you*. You will be challenged and confronted, no doubt. But you will also face your deepest desires in life and discover how those desires can be satisfied in the scandalous life of Jesus. My hope and prayer is that as you reflect on the problem of Jesus you will see how his life-changing claims have come to define our lives today.

MARK CLARK, author of *The Problem of Jesus*

How to Use
THIS GUIDE

The *Problem of Jesus* video study is designed to be experienced in a group setting such as a Bible study, Sunday school class, or any small group gathering. Each session begins with a welcome section, two questions to get you thinking about the topic, and a reading from the Bible. You will then watch a video with Mark Clark and engage in a small-group discussion. You will close each session with a time of personal reflection and prayer as a group.

Each person in the group should have a copy of this study guide and a Bible. Multiple translations will be used throughout the study, so whatever translation you have is fine. You are also encouraged to have a copy of *The Problem of Jesus* book, as reading it alongside the curriculum will provide you with deeper insights and make the journey more meaningful. (See the "For Next Week" section at the end of each between-studies section for the chapters in the book that correspond to material you and your group are discussing.)

> **Please Note:** The session material is longer than a typical small group study. If needed, you have the option to split each session into two parts: part A and part B. If you decide to cover each session in its entirety, please give ample time (at least two hours) to watch the video and work through the group discussion questions together.

To get the most out of your group experience, keep the following points in mind. First, the real growth in this study will happen during your small-group time. This is where you will process the content of the teaching for the week, ask questions, and learn from others as you hear what God is doing in their lives. For this reason, it is important for you to be fully committed to the group and attend each session so you can build trust and rapport with the other members. If you choose only to go through the motions, or if you refrain from participating, there is less of a chance you will find what you're looking for during this study.

Second, remember the goal of your small group is to serve as a place where people can share, learn about God, and build intimacy and friendship. For this reason, seek to make your group a safe place. This means being honest about your thoughts and feelings and listening carefully to everyone else's opinion. (If you are a group leader, there are additional instructions and resources in the back of the book for leading a productive discussion group.)

Third, resist the temptation to fix a problem someone might be having or to correct his or her theology, as that's not the purpose of your small-group time. Also, keep everything your group shares confidential. This will foster a rewarding sense of community in your group and create a place where people can heal, be challenged, and grow spiritually.

Following your group time, reflect on the material you've covered by engaging in the between-sessions activities. For each session, you may wish to complete the personal study all in one sitting or spread it out over a few. Note that if you are unable to finish (or even start!) your between-sessions personal study, you should still attend the group study video session. You are still wanted and welcome at the group even if you don't have your "homework" done.

Keep in mind the videos, discussion questions, and activities are simply meant to kick-start your thoughts so you are not only open to what God wants you to hear but also how to apply it to your life. As you go through this study, be open and listening to what God is saying to you as you discover an insightful, fresh perspective on *The Problem of Jesus*.

> **Note:** If you are a group leader, additional resources are provided in the back of this guide to help you lead your group members through the study.

The Problem of
THE HISTORICAL JESUS

*I must proclaim the good news of the kingdom
of God to the other towns also, because that is
why I was sent.*

—LUKE 4:43

Welcome

Today we're talking about the historical Jesus of Nazareth, one of the most interesting and influential figures in history. However, this session isn't just about Jesus; it's actually more about *you*. It's about what you do with the most important person who ever lived and how it defines your life. What we do with Jesus doesn't just define our lives in this moment—it defines the fate of everyone who has ever lived. Eternity hangs in the balance based on how we define and accept Jesus today. So, in this first session, we will see the first problem of Jesus is that he brings us to a crisis of faith, challenging us to either make him our center or deny him all together. In order to accept Jesus, we must first understand who he was and understand the meaning of his message, because without a proper understanding of Jesus and his context, we misunderstand him in small yet significant ways. When we see Jesus in his first-century Jewish context rather than our modern Western context, we see how his whole life—all he did and taught—comes alive in fresh and colorful ways. Jesus' ministry did what all good prophetic ministries do: it subverted the stories, beliefs, and actions of the existing religious movements and replaced them with something better. Jesus brought a kingdom message to his audience, and in doing so, he offered something scandalous for his time: *membership in the new people of God on his own authority and by his own process.* He did this by consciously putting himself in the role of Israel. Jesus made it clear that he was bringing Israel's history to a final phase and redrawing the boundary lines of Israel, including Jews and Gentiles alike. That's why looking at Jesus in his original context is so important, because it helps us guard against making Jesus in our own image and using him for our own agenda, and it helps us understand what his message actually was—what he was doing and saying, and *why*. So let's take a closer look at the problem of the historical Jesus.

Share

If you or any of your group members are just getting to know one another, take a few minutes to introduce yourselves. Then, to kick things off, briefly discuss one of the following:

- Share one hope or expectation you have for this study.

  —or—

- What are some common misconceptions we have about the historical nature of Jesus?

Read

Invite someone to read aloud the following Bible passage as preparation for Mark's teaching. Listen for fresh insights as you hear the verses being read, and then briefly discuss the questions that follow.

> *The Vine and the Branches*
>
> I am the true vine, and my Father is the gardener. He cuts off every branch in me that bears no fruit, while every branch that does bear fruit he prunes so that it will be even more fruitful. You are already clean because of the word I have spoken to you. Remain in me, as I also remain in you. No branch can bear fruit by itself; it must remain in the vine. Neither can you bear fruit unless you remain in me.
>
> I am the vine; you are the branches. If you remain in me and I in you, you will bear much fruit; apart from me you can do nothing. If you do not remain in me, you are like a branch that is thrown away and withers; such branches are picked up, thrown into the fire and burned. If you remain in me and my words remain in you, ask whatever you wish, and it will be done for you. This is to my Father's glory, that you bear much fruit, showing yourselves to be my disciples.

As the Father has loved me, so have I loved you. Now remain in my love. If you keep my commands, you will remain in my love, just as I have kept my Father's commands and remain in his love. I have told you this so that my joy may be in you and that your joy may be complete. My command is this: Love each other as I have loved you. Greater love has no one than this: to lay down one's life for one's friends. You are my friends if you do what I command. I no longer call you servants, because a servant does not know his master's business. Instead, I have called you friends, for everything that I learned from my Father I have made known to you. You did not choose me, but I chose you and appointed you so that you might go and bear fruit—fruit that will last—and so that whatever you ask in my name the Father will give you. This is my command: Love each other. (John 15:1–17)

What is one key insight that stands out to you from this passage?

_____

_____

_____

_____

Why is the vine and branches metaphor so significant for Jesus' audience?

_____

_____

_____

_____

Consider as you listen to Mark's teaching: *What would change about your perspective of the gospel if you understood the words of Jesus through the eyes and ears of a first-century Jew?*

_____

_____

_____

Watch ▶

Play the video segment for session 1. As you watch, use the following outline to record any thoughts or concepts that stand out to you.

NOTES: PART A

———— Did Jesus Really Exist? ————

What we do with Jesus defines the faith of everyone who has ever lived.

The *scandal* of Jesus

> But we preach Christ crucified: a stumbling block . . .
> —1 CORINTHIANS 1:23

"skandalon"(n)—original Greek

> ". . . and they took offense to him."
> —MATTHEW 13:57

Three kinds of people and responses to Jesus:

1. those who loved Jesus
2. those who rejected Jesus
3. those who were indifferent to Jesus

> A man who is merely a man and said the sorts of things Jesus said would not be a great moral teacher. He would either be a lunatic . . . or else he would be the Devil of Hell. . . . But let us not come with any patronizing nonsense about his being a great human teacher. He has not left that open to us.
> —C. S. LEWIS

There is no middle ground with Jesus.

———— The Challenges of Jesus ————

The study of the historical Jesus: *Did he exist and what was his message?*

Evidence of Jesus outside the Bible

- Ten different writers from history who talk about Jesus by name

Nero fastened the guilt on a class hated for their abominations called Christians by the populous. Christus, from whom the name had its origin, suffered the extreme penalty during the reign of Tiberius at the hand of Pontius Pilate.

—TACITUS

- The portrait we can construct of Jesus based on ancient writers:
    i. Jesus was a Jewish teacher
    ii. People believed he performed miracles and exorcisms
    iii. People believed he was the Messiah
    iv. He was tried and crucified under Pontius Pilate
    v. Despite his death, people actually worshiped him as God and said he rose from the dead

Evidence of Jesus within the Bible

- The Gospels: Matthew, Mark, Luke, and John
    The standard of historical investigation when applied to the Gospels actually shows the Gospels to be historically legitimate.

    When we compare the records of other religious figures in history: Zoroaster, Buddha, Muhammad, we have better historical documentation for the existence of Jesus than for any of those figures.

    —EDWIN YAMAUCHI

- The Gospels themselves reference:
    i. Hundreds of historical events
    ii. Geographical locations
    iii. Cites confirmed by archeological findings
    iv. Other historical personalities

    Many characters in the Gospels are unnamed, but others are named. I want to suggest now the possibility that many of these named characters were eyewitnesses who not only originated the traditions to which their names are attached but also continued to tell these stories as authoritative guarantors of their traditions.

    —RICHARD BAUCKHAM

Simon the Cyrene: ". . . the father of Alexander and Rufus" (Mark 15:21).

Bartimaeus: ". . . the son of Timaeus" (Mark 10:46).

> The writers name names because they expect their readers to personally know people within the stories that they're telling.
>
> —RICHARD BAUCKHAM

Evidence for Jesus in the Discrepancies and Contradictions of the Bible

- There is also credibility in the Gospels because of its discrepancies and contradictions.
  - i. The writers don't try to harmonize their information.

> For if that [the resurrection] were the fabrication of a congregation or of a similar group of people, then the tale would be consistently and obviously completely free of discrepancies.
>
> —HANS STIER

The reasons skeptics choose to not believe the Bible are actually cited by historians as reasons to believe it.

  - ii. The gospel writers include material that casts Jesus in a negative light.

> "Father, if you are willing, take this cup from me; yet not my will, but yours be done."
>
> —LUKE 22:42

  - iii. Women as eyewitnesses of the resurrection.

> He appeared to more than five hundred of the brothers and sisters at the same time, most of whom are still living, though some have fallen asleep.
>
> —1 CORINTHIANS 15:6

Evidence for Jesus in the Stories of Others

- The Gospels include more than thirty names of people who have been historically verified.

Evidence for Jesus in the **Persecution of the Early Church**

- Many people willingly suffered for their belief in Jesus as the Christ.

Key question: What was (and still is) the main message of Jesus?
Jump ahead to the group discussion if you're doing this session in two parts.

NOTES: PART B

————— **Why It Matters That Jesus** —————
Really Existed

Practice: Read the Gospels in light of first-century Judaism.

THE REAL MEANING OF JOHN 15

- *The vine*: an image for Israel . . . until Jesus.
- *The branch*: "Abide in me" means "to remain"—now it's about Jesus.
- Jesus was reframing.
- What we thought Jesus was saying might be different when he's understood in the light of first-century Judaism.

WHO WAS JESUS?

- His name means "God is salvation."
- He had four brothers and a number of sisters.
- He was part of the working class in a farming society.
- He was born in Bethlehem and grew up in Nazareth.
- He spent most of his life in ministry in Galilee and not in Judea, which was the center of religious life.

KEY QUESTIONS

What did Jesus say, teach, and do that so changed the world?
Why did Jesus die?
Why did Jesus live?

Jesus was a first-century Galilean Jew who spoke and lived like his contemporaries.

What Did Jesus Mean by What He Said?

- The twelve disciples—a symbolic reconstituting of the identity of the people of God
- Jesus' baptism and temptation (Mark 1:9–13; Matthew 2:15)
- The central salvation story of the Jews—the exodus story
- Jesus puts himself in the place of the people of God

What Was the Main Message of Jesus to the World?

- The kingdom of God

> "The time is fulfilled, and the kingdom of God is at hand; repent, and believe in the gospel."
>
> —MARK 1:15 RSV

> "I must preach the good news of the kingdom of God to the other cities also; for I was sent for this purpose."
>
> —LUKE 4:43 RSV

> The central aspect of the teaching of Jesus was that concerning the kingdom of God. All else in his message and ministry serves a function in relation to that proclamation and deriving its meaning from it.
>
> —NORMAN PERRIN

- Jesus announces the reign and the rule of God.
- Jesus addresses the fundamental questions of the universe and human life:
  - Is God in charge?
  - Who are God's people?

The entire life and ministry of Jesus is the announcement of the arrival of the kingdom of God.

> "But if it is by the finger of God that I cast out demons, then the kingdom of God has come upon you."
>
> —LUKE 11:20 RSV

Even the miracles and healings of Jesus were announcements to the world that God was breaking through the veil through the work of Jesus.

> Every physical healing pointed back to a time in Eden when physical bodies did not go blind, get crippled, or bleed nonstop for twelve years—and also pointed forward to a time of re-creation to come.
>
> —PHILIP YANCEY

The miracles and healings of Jesus were also about outsiders being restored and welcomed back into the new people of God.

> In addition to the physical burden of being blind, or lame, or deaf, or dumb, such a Jew was blemished, and unable to be a full Israelite.
>
> —N. T. WRIGHT

Jesus was spreading holiness and wholeness.

What Is It to Be a Christian?

- To become someone who embraces the rulership of God over their life through the person and work of Jesus

> God's plan was not to save souls apart from history but to bring the kingdom of God into the world with explosive force.
>
> —MARK CLARK

- The call to conversion: to be converted to Christ means to give one's allegiance to the kingdom of God.

  Jesus was offering something far more scandalous: membership in the new people of God based on his own authority and by his own process.

KEY QUESTIONS

- *Are you willing to give your life to the one who creates the scandal in this world?*
- *Who is your master?*
- *Which kingdom do you belong to?*

Group Discussion

Take a few minutes to discuss what you just watched and explore these concepts in Scripture.

PART A

1. What stood out to you from Mark's teaching on the historical evidence of Jesus?

   _____

   _____

   _____

   _____

   _____

2. What is so convincing about the evidence that Jesus really did exist? And why does it matter?

   _____

   _____

   _____

   _____

3. **Read Mark 1:9–13.** As Mark mentioned, have you ever considered the baptism and temptation of Jesus in light of the exodus story? How does this change the way you see these significant events in the life of Jesus?

   _____

   _____

   _____

   _____

4. **Read Matthew 9:18–38 and Mark 5:21–43.** These are two different perspectives of the same stories, plus a few more miracles performed by Jesus. What was so significant about the miracles and healings of Jesus? How did the wholeness Jesus brought to people who were sick and dying highlight his holiness?

   _____

   _____

   _____

If you're doing session 1 in two parts, pause your discussion here. Take time to pray together as a group. Use the space at the end of this session to keep track of prayer requests and group updates. Otherwise, continue answering the questions for part B of your group discussion.

PART B

5. **Read Matthew 2:1–15.** How were the details of Jesus' escape to Egypt significant to a first-century Jew? How does this passage build a bridge between the exodus of the Israelites and the life of Jesus?

_____

_____

_____

_____

_____

6. **Read Luke 4:42–44.** According to Jesus, what is the good news of the kingdom of God? What does this passage mean for you?

_____

_____

_____

_____

7. When you view Jesus in light of the scandal he created with his presence in the world, what is it about Jesus that makes you want to follow him?

_____

_____

_____

_____

8. How would you honestly answer this question today: *Who is your master, and which kingdom do you belong to—the world or the kingdom of heaven?*

_____

_____

_____

_____

Pray

Pray as a group before you close your time together. Ask God to open your hearts and minds and allow you to see Jesus as the first-century Jew that he was when we walked the earth. Ask God to illuminate your perspective on Jesus so that you no longer have a problem explaining the historical Jesus from your perspective. Use this space to keep track of prayer requests and group updates.

Between-Sessions
PERSONAL STUDY

Weekly Reflection

Before you begin the between-sessions exercises, briefly review your video notes for session 1. In the space below, write down the *most significant point* you took away from this session.

_____

_____

_____

_____

_____

_____

_____

_____

_____

_____

_____

_____

Take some time to reflect on the material you covered during your group time by engaging in any or all of the following between-sessions exercises. These exercises follow the flow of the group experience with two exercises per each part of this session. As you read and experience the material, you may want to make a few notes in your guide. The primary goal of these between-sessions exercises is for your own spiritual growth and personal reflection, and it is not a requirement for group participation. *Note: the verses to read have most likely appeared in other areas of this session as well, but they are placed in these exercises for intentional reflection.* If you haven't done so already, read chapters 1 and 2 in *The Problem of Jesus*.

Part A

Day 1: The Kingdom of God through Jesus
Read: *Matthew 28:22–37; Mark 1:1–15; 4:10–12*

Consider: We now understand that Jesus' primary identity was that of a prophet proclaiming the arrival of the kingdom of God. But what did Jesus actually mean by "the kingdom of God"? Once we locate Jesus in his first-century Jewish context, we come to realize that Jesus was referring to the reign or rule of God and how it was playing out in relationship to the world. This wasn't just about "going to heaven when we die." Through artistic suggestiveness, Jesus was telling a story that included God's creation, the corruption of that creation by human sin, the choosing of Israel to restore the world, the slavery of God's chosen people, the exodus, and the promised land. By the time we get to Jesus, he connects his life and ministry and the fulfillment of God's kingdom to earlier expectations, set out in earlier scenes. Jesus was God breaking through to reign in the world through the forgiveness of sins, the defeat of evil, the end of exile, and the return of God to God's people. Jesus' life and ministry were nothing less than the announcement of the arrival of a *new world*—and he was boldly saying that he was ushering it in.

Reflect: Take a few moments to reflect on your answers to these questions.

What does it mean, in your own words, for Jesus to usher in the kingdom of God?

_____

_____

_____

_____

Why does Jesus' life matter just as much as his death?

_____

_____

_____

Why does Jesus matter to you?

_____

_____

_____

Pray: Close your time today by praying to God. Pray whatever comes to mind as you consider these passages and these questions.

Day 2: How Jesus Draws Us into the Kingdom
Read: *Isaiah 35:5–6; 53:1–6; Matthew 11:5*

Consider: The healings of Jesus listed throughout the New Testament served a purpose greater than illustrating his divinity or his desire to "help people." The healings were Jesus' announcement to the world that God was breaking through the veil in a special way. The healings were an indication that this great kingdom moment finally had arrived. They were more than the restoration of sick people; they were symbolic of outsiders being fully restored and welcomed into the people of God. In a day and age where there were laws and customs about separation between the "clean" and "unclean," anyone with a disability or illness was avoided. Jesus shattered this orientation, as he interacted with all kinds of "unclean" people and healed their afflictions. Jesus was spreading holiness and wholeness, as well as redrawing the lines around membership in the people of God. The expectation of restored land that the Jews were waiting for, Jesus was now defining as a restored *people*. Still today, Jesus draws the human race into the kingdom of God by healing our wounds and cleansing our hearts.

Reflect: Take a few moments to reflect on your answers to these questions.

What is symbolic and meaningful about the healings of Jesus?

_____

_____

_____

_____

Why is it important that Jesus not only brings the kingdom of God to earth but also draws humanity into the kingdom of God with his actions and words?

_____

_____

_____

_____

_____

How do you need to be healed by Jesus?

_____

_____

_____

_____

_____

Pray: Close your time today by praying to God. Pray whatever comes to mind as you consider these passages and these questions.

Part B

> **Day 3:** What Does It Mean to Be a Christian?
> **Read:** *Mark 2:1–12; Luke 7:36–50; 15:11–32*

Consider: If we limit ourselves to a Western, individualized sense of forgiveness in the stories of Jesus, then we miss the big picture. If we notice that Jesus is necessary for the forgiveness of sinners, and we understand the story of ancient Israel in the Old Testament, then we see that there is a need for personal ransom to save sinners. This was always central to the expectations of ancient Israel and to the stories of forgiveness told by Jesus. In context, these stories are signs that *all people* willing to come under the rule of God through the person and work of Jesus are welcome—no matter the geography or ethnicity of a person. To become a "Christian" then is to become someone who embraces the rulership of God through the person and work of Jesus. And this applies to every area of our lives: our souls, our thoughts, our finances, our intimate relationships, our families, our jobs, our community engagement, and so on. To be a Christian is to submit to the reign of God in our lives.

Reflect: Take a few moments to reflect on your answers to these questions.

What does it mean for you to be a Christian?

_____

_____

_____

_____

_____

Why does following Jesus matter to you?

_____

_____

_____

_____

How does your life reflect a holistic perspective of surrender to the reign of God in your life?

_____

_____

_____

_____

Pray: Close your time today by praying to God. Pray whatever comes to mind as you consider these passages and these questions.

Day 4: The Difference between Jesus and Paul
Read: *Matthew 28:18–20; Mark 1:14–15; Romans 7; Ephesians 2:8–10*

Consider: Skeptics are quick to point out the difference between the teachings of Paul and the teachings of Jesus, often questioning whether or not the two contradict one another on topics such as the kingdom of God and faith versus works. But any differences between the two can be attributed to the idea that Jesus was declaring the arrival of the kingdom of God, and Paul was applying the implications of such a reality to local churches and their mission in the world. Jesus was declaring the kingdom, while Paul was declaring the King. Just as John the Baptist was preparing the way for Jesus, Paul was clearing doubt out of the way regarding Jesus as the Messiah and King among first-century Jews and the early church.

Reflect:

Why is it important to understand the varying contexts of Jesus and Paul as we read their words in Scripture?

_____

_____

_____

_____

Why did Paul dedicate his life to declaring that Jesus was King?

_____

_____

_____

_____

How am I dedicating my life to declaring Jesus as King?

_____

_____

_____

_____

Pray: Close your time today by praying to God. Pray whatever comes to mind as you consider these passages and these questions.

For Next Week: Read chapters 3 and 4 in *The Problem of Jesus* and use the space below to write any insights or questions from your personal study that you want to discuss at the next group meeting.

_____

_____

_____

_____

_____

Journal, Reflections, and Notes

_____

_____

_____

_____

_____

_____

_____

The Problem of
THE GOSPELS

*I came that they may have life, and have it
abundantly.*

—JOHN 10:10 RSV

Welcome

Today we're talking about the problem of the Gospels. This may catch some of you by surprise, but Jesus probably did not actually say some of the most "famous" passages in the Bible that are commonly ascribed to him today—the passages and phrases we see on posters in sports stadiums or read as a benediction at the end of a sermon. *But isn't this what the skeptics usually say? And does this mean the Gospels can't be trusted?* It means, we need to start reading the Gospels more closely and more according to what the Gospels claim to be, versus what we try to make them into for our modern audiences. As Christians, it's easy to grow familiar with the Bible and tend to see what we want to see. But we miss so much about the teachings, messages, and meanings of Jesus if we do that—especially with the Gospels. When seen and understood as part of the ancient world, the Gospels become so rich that they never lose their effect on us. But we have to be open to a fresh perspective and a new "old" way of seeing the Gospels in order for their effect to translate into understanding, impact, and action at our end. In fact, the Gospels are bold, strategic stories with theological intent—even in the way they are organized. In them, we see the life and death of Jesus displayed in an astounding record that cared for both history and theology without compromising on either. But the question remains: *Do we trust the Gospels and what they say about Jesus, or do we remain skeptical?* Let's dig a little deeper together as we look at the problem of the Gospels.

Share 💬

If you or any of your group members are just getting to know one another, take a few minutes to introduce yourselves. Then, to kick things off, briefly discuss one of the following statements:

- Name a few common critiques we hear about the Bible from unbelievers today.

  —*or*—

- Do you trust what the Bible has to say about Jesus, or do you have some doubts? If it's the latter, share one doubt with the group.

Read 📖

Invite someone to read aloud the following passage as preparation for Mark's teaching. Listen for fresh insights as you hear the verses being read, and then briefly discuss the questions that follow.

Jesus Heals a Blind Man at Bethsaida

They came to Bethsaida, and some people brought a blind man and begged Jesus to touch him. He took the blind man by the hand and led him outside the village. When he had spit on the man's eyes and put his hands on him, Jesus asked, "Do you see anything?"

He looked up and said, "I see people; they look like trees walking around."

Once more Jesus put his hands on the man's eyes. Then his eyes were opened, his sight was restored, and he saw everything clearly. Jesus sent him home, saying, "Don't even go into the village."

Jesus and his disciples went on to the villages around Caesarea Philippi. On the way he asked them, "Who do people say I am?"

They replied, "Some say John the Baptist; others say Elijah; and still others, one of the prophets."

"But what about you?" he asked. "Who do you say I am?"

Peter answered, "You are the Messiah."

Jesus warned them not to tell anyone about him.

He then began to teach them that the Son of Man must suffer many things and be rejected by the elders, the chief priests and the teachers of the law, and that he must be killed and after three days rise again. He spoke plainly about this, and Peter took him aside and began to rebuke him.

But when Jesus turned and looked at his disciples, he rebuked Peter. "Get behind me, Satan!" he said. "You do not have in mind the concerns of God, but merely human concerns."

Then he called the crowd to him along with his disciples and said: "Whoever wants to be my disciple must deny themselves and take up their cross and follow me. For whoever wants to save their life will lose it, but whoever loses their life for me and for the gospel will save it. What good is it for someone to gain the whole world, yet forfeit their soul? Or what can anyone give in exchange for their soul? If anyone is ashamed of me and my words in this adulterous and sinful generation, the Son of Man will be ashamed of them when he comes in his Father's glory with the holy angels." (Mark 8:22–38)

What is one key insight that stands out to you from this passage?

_____

_____

_____

_____

What is so significant about the reality that the blind man was not fully healed the first time Jesus touched him? Why do you think Mark includes this passage?

_____

_____

_____

_____

Consider as you listen to Mark's teaching: *What would change about your perspective of this passage in Mark if you understood the words of Jesus through the eyes and ears of a first-century Gentile or Jew?*

_____

_____

_____

Watch ▶

Play the video segment for session 2. As you watch, use the following outline to record any thoughts or concepts that stand out to you.

NOTES: PART A

——— How to Read the Gospels Right ———

Shadow vs. reality

> You search the scriptures, because you think that in them you have eternal life; and it is they that bear witness to me; yet you refuse to come to me that you may have life. I do not receive glory from men. But I know that you have not the love of God within you. I have come in my Father's name, and you do not receive me; if another comes in his own name, him you will receive. How can you believe, who receive glory from one another and do not seek the glory that comes from the only God?
>
> —JOHN 5:39–44 RSV

We have to understand what the Gospels are giving us:

- Truth
- Facts
- "Truth on fire" (Martyn Lloyd-Jones)

——— Understanding What the Gospels *Are* and What They *Aren't* ———

The Gospels *are:*

- Four books—Matthew, Mark, Luke, and John
- Recognized collectively as the authoritative biographies of Jesus
- How we understand Jesus—the man, the message, the ministry

Two Key Questions to Understanding the Gospels

- *What are they?*
- *Can we trust them?*

> The best way to understand the writings called the Gospels, literally "good news," is as theological history.
>
> —MARK CLARK

——— The Bible as Theological History ———

- Greek-style biographies—fact-based stories
- Genre of Jewish storytelling—a prophet or teacher in light of anointing by God and God's message for the world
- Both methods prioritize the accurate retelling of facts through engaging storytelling
- Creative blend of history and theology

The Gospels are not biographies—they do not include every detail of Jesus' life.

> Ancient biographers and historians did not feel constrained to write from detached and so-called objective viewpoints. They did not give equal treatment to all periods of an individual's life. They felt free to write in topical as well as chronological sequence. They were highly selective in the material they included. . . . Words were abbreviated, explained, paraphrased and contemporized in whatever ways individual authors deemed beneficial for the audiences.
>
> —CRAIG BLOMBERG

The Gospels have a liberty based on the time they were written and the kind of thing they're presenting.

For example:

- Matthew: The kingdom of heaven (with a Jewish audience in mind)
- Mark and Luke: The kingdom of God

> For God so loved the world that he gave his only Son, that whoever believes in him should not perish but have eternal life.
>
> —JOHN 3:16 RSV

There was a different standard for stories in the ancient world of Jesus' day:

- Writers had the freedom to move stories around in support of the author's theological goal.
- Stories do not have to maintain chronology and tell everything in a certain order.

- The Gospel of Mark clusters the "miracle" stories in chapter 1 and the "parable" stories in chapter 4.

> Understanding the flexibility available to the gospel writers and the intentional way with which they ordered all of their events and stories actually opens up the Bible to us in amazing ways.
>
> —MARK CLARK

For example, *a blind man in Mark* 8:

- Jesus is asking the question to the man and the readers: *Do you really see, or do you only half-see?*
- Jesus is asking the question to the disciples: *What do the disciples actually understand about Jesus?*
- Jesus is asking the question to his greater audience, including us: *What do people understand theologically in their hearts?*

Reading ancient texts by modern standards is *chronological snobbery* (C. S. Lewis).

The Gospels are a product of their time.

Matthew, Mark, Luke, and John

> Each of these Gospels, in its own unique way, is trying to depict the life of Jesus as like the climax to Israel's story.
>
> —N. T. WRIGHT

MATTHEW

- Jesus is Emmanuel (chapter 1)
- The Great Commission (chapter 28)
- Jesus on mountains—Jesus as the new Moses, bringing about a new way
  - Five major blocks of Jesus' teaching
  - The Sermon on the Mount—the summary of what Jesus was trying to teach (chapters 5–7)

MARK

- The gospel for people in a hurry
- Includes parables, healings
- Eight chapters on the first years of Jesus' life
- Eight chapters on the last few weeks of Jesus' life
- Jesus shown in light of Isaiah

LUKE

- Writes two volumes—the Gospel of Luke (historical presentation of Jesus) and the book of Acts (historical presentation of the church)
- Was a doctor—researched, talked to eyewitnesses, presented Jesus in light of good history

JOHN

- Gets into the meaning of the good news
- Uses spiritual imagery
- Frequently uses "everlasting" or "eternal life" instead of "kingdom of God"

But can we trust them?

Jump ahead to the group discussion if you're doing this session in two parts.

NOTES: PART B

Trusting the Gospels and their legitimacy.

——— Criteria for the "Historicity" of the Gospels of the Bible ———

1. *The criteria of embarrassment*: we keep things that Jesus said and did that were embarrassing to the culture.
   - The way Jesus talks to his mother (John 2).
   - Applied to the writers themselves as a less-compelling group:
     - Mark and Luke were not even one of the twelve disciples.
     - Luke is obscure, mentioned by name only once in the New Testament.
     - Mark abandons Paul and, most likely, Jesus (Mark 14:51).
     - Matthew was a tax collector.
     - John's historicity gets challenged because it's so unlike the other Gospels.

2. The criteria of the stuff we never find in the Gospels.
   - There are still questions about controversial issues such as: circumcision, food laws, modes of baptism, speaking in tongues, spiritual gifts, the role of women in ministry.
3. The criteria of the differences of the Gospels.

> The overwhelming probability is that most of what Jesus said, he said not twice, but two hundred times with, of course, a myriad of local variations.
>
> —N. T. WRIGHT

- The stilling of the storm—Mark and Luke
- The healing of the possessed boy—Mark and Matthew
- The widow's might—Mark and Luke
- The Lord's Prayer—Matthew and Luke
- The Lord's Supper—Matthew and Mark
- The resurrection story—in each Gospel

If the Gospels were the fabrication of the early church, they would be completely free of discrepancies.

> The fact that they cannot agree over how many women, or angels, were at the tomb, or even on the location of the appearances, does not mean that nothing happened. But that the opposite is the case, actually—that something likely did. The stories exhibit exactly the surface tension which we associate not with tales artfully told by people eager to sustain a fiction, and therefore anxious to make everything look just right. But with hurried puzzled accounts of those who have seen with their own eyes something which took them horribly by surprise.
>
> —N. T. WRIGHT

External Evidence

- The gospel writers go out of their way to root themselves in history rather than spin legends.

> Inasmuch as many have undertaken to compile a narrative of the things which have been accomplished among us, just as they were delivered to us by those who

from the beginning were eyewitnesses and ministers of the word, it seemed good to me also, having followed all things closely for some time past, to write an orderly account for you.

—LUKE 1:1–3 RSV

- Luke references seven rulers from history (Luke 3).
- The details of Luke's account are confirmed by Josephus.
- Luke identifies thirty-two countries, fifty-four cities, and nine islands without error.

Archaeological work has unquestionably strengthened confidence in the reliability of the scriptural record.

—MILLAR BURROWS

Archaeological Evidence

- The tribute penny (Mark 12)
- The thirty pieces of silver (Matthew 26)
- The widow's might (Luke 21)

The Dating of the Gospels: Are They Legends?

- The abrupt ending of Acts
- Luke was written before Acts
- Mark (early 60s AD) and Matthew were both written before Luke

This adds up to a strong case that all three Gospels were composed within about thirty years of Jesus' death and well within the period of time when people could check up on the accuracy of the facts they contained.

—CRAIG BLOMBERG

Eyewitnesses of Jesus and his resurrection were still alive when the Gospels were written. **This is why you can trust the Gospels are true.**

——— Here's Why This Matters ———

Be courageous enough to face facts rather than taking the easy way out with denial.

> You search the scriptures, because you think that in them you have eternal life; and it is they that bear witness to me; yet you refuse to come to me that you may have life.
>
> —JOHN 5:39–40 RSV

We're all seeking eternal life—*abundant life*.

> I came that they may have life, and have it abundantly.
>
> —JOHN 10:10 RSV

Scholars are looking to the Bible for meaning and fulfillment (John 5).

——— The Problem of the Gospels: ———
We Gain Knowledge *about* God but Not *of* God

We need to understand the Word behind the Word (to paraphrase Karl Barth).

KEY QUESTIONS

- *Are we settling for print instead of the person in our lives?*
- *Are we settling for rules instead of relationship?*
- *Are we settling for letter instead of spirit?*
- *And why do we do this?*

> How can you believe, who receive glory from one another and do not seek the glory that comes from the only God?
>
> —JOHN 5:44 RSV

Pride and fear keep us from opening up our hearts to Jesus.
We all seek eternal life—a fuller way—offered by Jesus.
We can trust the Gospels as they point to Jesus and the faith we place in him.

Group Discussion

Take a few minutes to discuss what you just watched and explore these concepts in Scripture.

PART A

1. What stood out to you from Mark's teaching on the problem of the Gospels?

_____

_____

_____

_____

2. What is so convincing about the evidence of the Gospels' "historicity"?

_____

_____

_____

_____

3. **Read John 5:31–47.** What's so significant about the way Jesus talks to his witnesses here? Why is it important that Jesus mentioned John the Baptist in this passage?

_____

_____

_____

_____

4. **Read Matthew 5:1–12.** What does Mark mean when he says this passage in Matthew is the summary of what Jesus was trying to teach? How might this summary also reflect Matthew's perspective on the importance of Jesus' teachings?

_____

_____

_____

If you're doing session 2 in two parts, pause your discussion here. Take time to pray together as a group. Use the space at the end of this session to keep track of prayer requests and group updates. Otherwise, continue answering the questions for part B of your group discussion.

PART B

5. What stands out to you about the criteria used to determine the historicity of the Gospels: *embarrassment, the stuff we can't find,* and *the differences between perspectives and stories*? Give a brief example from Scripture in one of these three areas.

    _____

    _____

    _____

    _____

    _____

6. **Read Luke 1:1–4 and Luke 3.** How does knowing that Luke was a physician shape the way we experience his Gospel? Why was it important to Luke to list the genealogy of Jesus?

    _____

    _____

    _____

    _____

    _____

7. **Read the resurrection story in Matthew 28; Mark 16; Luke 24:1–49; and John 20.** What differences do you notice in the way these stories are told?

    _____

    _____

    _____

    _____

    _____

8. How does the evidence of the Bible, especially what you know about the Gospels, shape your personal relationship with Jesus? And how does the evidence of the Bible shape the way you reflect on Scripture as a church community?

    _____

    _____

    _____

    _____

Pray

Pray as a group before you close your time together. Thank God for the evidence that allows us to trust the Gospels as they point to Jesus. Ask God to continue to show you the gift of abundant life offered to us through the story and sacrifice of Jesus. May we see the Gospels as they were intended—as theological history—instead of through the filter of our modern lens. Use this space to keep track of prayer requests and group updates.

Between-Sessions
PERSONAL STUDY

Weekly Reflection

Before you begin the between-sessions exercises, briefly review your video notes for session 2. In the space below, write down the *most significant point* you took away from this session.

_____

_____

_____

_____

_____

_____

_____

_____

_____

_____

Take some time to reflect on the material you covered during your group time by engaging in any or all of the following between-sessions exercises. These exercises follow the flow of the group experience with two exercises per each part of this session. As you read and experience the material, you may want to make a few notes in your guide. The primary goal of these between-sessions exercises is for your own spiritual growth and personal reflection, and it is not a requirement for group participation. *Note: the verses to read have most likely appeared in other areas of this session as well, but they are placed in these exercises for intentional reflection.* If you haven't done so already, read chapters 3 and 4 in *The Problem of Jesus*.

Part A

Day 1: The Good News according to Matthew

Read: *Matthew 1:1–14; 5–7; and 28:16–20 (or read the entire Gospel if you have the time)*

Consider: Each of the Gospels, in its own way, depicts the life of Jesus as the climax to Israel's story. The Gospel of Matthew was written in the AD 60s–70s and is most likely written to a Jewish audience. Matthew presents Jesus as the fulfillment of an earlier story, and this is why his gospel begins with a genealogy that seems to reshape the genealogy of Genesis. However, the story written by Mathew is of a "new creation." Matthew connects the life of Jesus to the story of Abraham, Isaac, and Jacob and mentions Jesus as the new and even better Moses. Matthew mentions the story of Israel in exile and slavery under a foreign pagan power—once Egypt, now Rome. And he writes about the Israelites waiting for a savior to come and take them to the promised land. Jesus gives Matthew's audience a new covenant and a new way to live through the Sermon on the Mount and four other blocks of teaching found in Matthew 10; 13; 18; and 23–25. Matthew leaves his readers with the great commission of Jesus in Matthew 28:16–20.

Reflect: Take a few moments to reflect on your answers to these questions.

What stands out to you about the way Matthew tells the good news of Jesus?

_____

_____

_____

What seems to be unique about Matthew's perspective on Jesus?

_____

_____

_____

How might this particular gospel create a crisis of faith for first-century Jews? How does it create a crisis of faith for you or challenge you to change?

_____

_____

_____

Pray: Close your time today by praying to God. Pray whatever comes to mind as you consider these passages and these questions.

Day 2: The Good News according to Mark
Read: *Isaiah 40:1–11; Mark 1:1–8; and 4:10–13*

Consider: Mark's gospel is believed to be the earliest, written somewhere between the mid-40s and early 60s AD. Mark presents a "new exodus" reality but not directly according to the book of Exodus because he never makes that linguistic connection. However, he does reference the fulfillment of a new exodus as presented in Isaiah, citing Isaiah in every chapter. He starts the gospel story by giving us the story of Jesus "according to Isaiah." Mark also presents Jesus as the suffering servant from Isaiah 40–55 and as the new Moses with Jesus feeding Israel in the desert and grouping them like Moses did. To understand Mark is to understand Isaiah. So if you have time, read through the key passages of Isaiah too.

Reflect: Take a few moments to reflect on your answers to these questions.

What stands out to you about the way Mark tells the good news of Jesus?

_____

_____

_____

_____

What seems to be unique about Mark's perspective on Jesus?

_____

_____

_____

How might Mark's gospel create a crisis of faith for first-century Jews? How does it create a crisis of faith for you or challenge you to change?

_____

_____

_____

Pray: Close your time today by praying to God. Pray whatever comes to mind as you consider these passages and these questions.

Part B

Day 3: The Good News according to Luke
Read: *1 Samuel 1–2; Luke 1*

Consider: Luke is the third gospel, written in the late 50s or early 60s AD, and it centers around the creation of Israel's monarchy, starting with the story of Elizabeth and Zechariah, which is intended to point readers back to the story of Hannah and Elkanah (1 Samuel 1–2). The stories take similar shapes and result in similarly triumphant conclusions. This is why both Mary and Zechariah sing Hannah's song. The story in 1 Samuel follows the challenging journey and kingly climax of the life of David. The parallels continue in the anointing of David and Jesus as the representatives of Israel, and both stories are followed by battles with the giants of their day, Goliath and Satan. In many ways, to know the story of David is to know the story of Jesus.

Reflect: Take a few moments to reflect on your answers to these questions.

What stands out to you about the way Luke tells the good news of Jesus?

_____

_____

_____

_____

What seems to be unique about Luke's perspective on Jesus?

_____

_____

_____

How might Luke's gospel create a crisis of faith for first-century Jews? How does it create a crisis of faith for you or challenge you to change?

_____

_____

_____

Pray: Close your time today by praying to God. Pray whatever comes to mind as you consider these passages and these questions.

Day 4: The Good News according to John
Read: *John 1:1–18; 2:25–59; Exodus 16*

Consider: John is the fourth and last gospel, written in the AD 90s, and it stands apart from the rest as it represents Jesus in more of a mystical way in the words, images, ideas, and stories shared by the writer. There's a good chance John knew the other gospel writers and their works and wanted to present Jesus in a different way. Although similar to the other gospel writers, John also seems to reflect on an earlier story by mirroring the themes and structure of Genesis. John consistently gives more detail and references to time, place, and physical descriptions than any of the gospel writers. Despite past scrutiny of the historical trustworthiness of John's account, it is because of John that we know Jesus had at least a three-year ministry. And it is because of John's detailed account that we have archaeological evidence to support the stories mentioned in his gospel.

Reflect: Take a few moments to reflect on your answers to these questions.

What stands out to you about the way John tells the good news of Jesus?

_____

_____

_____

_____

What seems to be unique about John's perspective on Jesus?

_____

_____

_____

How might John's gospel create a crisis of faith for first-century Jews? How does it create a crisis of faith for you or challenge you to change?

_____

_____

_____

Pray: Close your time today by praying to God. Pray whatever comes to mind as you consider these passages and these questions.

For Next Week: Read chapters 5 and 6 in *The Problem of Jesus* and use the space below to write any insights or questions from your personal study that you want to discuss at the next group meeting.

_____

_____

_____

_____

_____

_____

Journal, Reflections, and Notes

_____

_____

_____

_____

_____

_____

_____

_____

_____

_____

_____

_____

_____

_____

_____

_____

_____

_____

The Problem of
DISCIPLESHIP

Then Jesus said to his disciples, "Whoever wants to be my disciple must deny themselves and take up their cross and follow me."

—MATTHEW 16:24

Welcome

Some popular religious writers today claim that Jesus was a great guy, a moral teacher, a visionary, an inspiring leader, an archetype, or a religious guru—but not God. The call to follow Jesus, they would say, is too fanatical, too devoted and naive. There's a vision of a good life for us—made easier and better—and our hearts buy into these ideas of a better life far too often. This is the problem of discipleship. For people in the first-century, they were looking for vision, inspiration, personal and political revolution. Jesus *offered* them something, but he *asked* something of them too. He says if we want to save our lives, we will lose them, but if we're willing to lose our lives, he will save them. And Jesus asks us if we're willing to deny ourselves, take up our cross, and follow him (Mark 8). This is his threefold invitation and his call to discipleship. While this invitation and call may appear to be the worst strategy for pursuing our personal fulfillment, they may actually be the best thing for us. That's why we're going to look into what would motivate anyone to take Jesus up on his vision of following him on a long, difficult journey of self-denial. This is the problem of discipleship.

Share 💬

To kick things off, briefly discuss one of the following statements:

- Name something *good* you've given up in the present for something *greater* that you hope to receive in the future.

  —*or*—

- What does the word *discipleship* mean to you?

Read 📖

Invite someone to read aloud the following passage as preparation for Mark's teaching. Listen for fresh insights as you hear the verses being read, and then briefly discuss the questions that follow.

> *The Rich and the Kingdom of God*
>
> Just then a man came up to Jesus and asked, "Teacher, what good thing must I do to get eternal life?"
>
> "Why do you ask me about what is good?" Jesus replied. "There is only One who is good. If you want to enter life, keep the commandments."
>
> "Which ones?" he inquired.
>
> Jesus replied, "'You shall not murder, you shall not commit adultery, you shall not steal, you shall not give false testimony, honor your father and mother,' and 'love your neighbor as yourself.'"
>
> "All these I have kept," the young man said. "What do I still lack?"
>
> Jesus answered, "If you want to be perfect, go, sell your possessions and give to the poor, and you will have treasure in heaven. Then come, follow me."
>
> When the young man heard this, he went away sad, because he had great wealth.
>
> Then Jesus said to his disciples, "Truly I tell you, it is hard for someone who is rich to enter the kingdom of heaven. Again I tell you, it is easier for a camel to go through the eye of a needle than for someone who is rich to enter the kingdom of God."
>
> When the disciples heard this, they were greatly astonished and asked, "Who then can be saved?"
>
> Jesus looked at them and said, "With man this is impossible, but with God all things are possible."

Peter answered him, "We have left everything to follow you! What then will there be for us?"

Jesus said to them, "Truly I tell you, at the renewal of all things, when the Son of Man sits on his glorious throne, you who have followed me will also sit on twelve thrones, judging the twelve tribes of Israel. And everyone who has left houses or brothers or sisters or father or mother or wife or children or fields for my sake will receive a hundred times as much and will inherit eternal life. But many who are first will be last, and many who are last will be first." (Matthew 19:16–30)

What is one key insight that stands out to you from this passage?

_____

_____

_____

_____

_____

_____

_____

Why did the rich young ruler go away sad?

_____

_____

_____

_____

_____

_____

_____

What is the cost of following Jesus?

_____

_____

_____

_____

_____

Watch ▶️

Play the video segment for session 3. As you watch, use the following outline to record any thoughts or concepts that stand out to you.

NOTES: PART A

——— The Problem of Discipleship Is Understanding Not Only ——— What Jesus *Asks* but Also What Jesus *Offers*

"Whoever wants to be my disciple must deny themselves and take up their cross and follow me. For whoever wants to save their life will lose it, but whoever loses their life for me and for the gospel will save it."

—MARK 8:34–35

Jesus motivates us with self-denial.
Key question: Then why would we want to follow Jesus?

"If you are the Son of God," he said, "throw yourself down." (verse 6)
   "All this I will give you," he said, "if you will bow down and worship me." (verse 9)
   "If you are the Son of God, tell these stones to become bread." (verse 3)

—MATTHEW 4

Jesus knew that the devil always presents to us on a temporal level something God has promised on an eternal level.

—ERIC MASON

"All authority in heaven and on earth has been given to me."

—MATTHEW 28:18

The devil wanted to give [Jesus] earthly kingdoms, but God wanted to give [Jesus] all kingdoms.

—ERIC MASON

We cannot have the kingdoms of the world *and* still have authority in heaven.

The devil will try to make you believe that God does not have "better" for you. Jesus suffered for a *purpose*.

> For the joy set before him he endured the cross, scorning its shame, and sat down at the right hand of the throne of God. Consider him who endured such opposition from sinners, so that you will not grow weary and lose heart.
>
> —HEBREWS 12:2–3

We must pursue a greater good in God.

> Long ago in the dim mists of time, we as human beings, began to realize that reality was structured as if it could be bargained with. We learned that behaving properly now, in the present, regulating our impulses, considering the plight of others, could actually bring rewards in the future, in a time and place that did not yet exist.
>
> —JORDAN PETERSON

—— Following Jesus ——

The secret to following Jesus: *sacrifice now to gain later.*
The apocalyptic perspective of Jesus: *a future view which enabled him in his present life.*
This perspective is often ignored in our modern world.

> I consider that our present sufferings are not worth comparing with the glory that will be revealed in us.
>
> —ROMANS 8:18

KEY QUESTIONS

How can we follow Jesus?
How can we deny ourselves?
How can we pick up our cross daily?
How can we live a life of sacrifice?

Because we know a better life is on its way for the rest of eternity. The cost is worth it.

We often lack faith that the future Jesus promises us is real, and it's better than what we can experience here and now.

Discipleship Is a *Human* Thing, Not Just a Christian Thing

The Greek word for "disciple" is *mathētēs*, which means "learner." We are all disciples in one form or another.

Who or What Are You Following?

At the heart level, we need to change *what we love*:

- Our beliefs
- Our habits (actions, behaviors)
- Our desires (see Matthew 9:36)

Then How Should We Live?

Our lives must look different if we are following Christ

The Call of Discipleship Is Costly

It's a reprioritization of everything:

- Relationships
- Money
- Work
- Family life

The rich young ruler couldn't walk away from his life, so he walked away from Jesus (Mark 10:17–31).

> The default setting of the human heart is a rejection of Jesus' authority over our lives.
> —MARK CLARK

Jesus' remedy for this rejection:

- Deny yourself.
- Pick up your cross.
- Follow me.

These are the invitations of Jesus to discipleship in him.

Jump ahead to the group discussion if you're doing this session in two parts.

NOTES: PART B

——— **The Three Invitations of Jesus** ———

1. Deny yourself.
   - This is countercultural.
   - Jesus knows that if we look for what we *want*, we will never be satisfied.
   - The human heart is drawn to things that are part of the problem—trying to find meaning and joy in the wrong places.
   - We are not the heroes of our stories.

   > "For whoever wants to save their life will lose it, but whoever loses their life for me and for the gospel will save it."
   > —MARK 8:35

   > The deliberately chosen Greek word for "life" here is *psychē*, from which we get our word *psychology*. It denotes your identity, your personality, your selfhood.
   > —TIM KELLER

   > Self-emptiness readies us for fullness.
   > —MARK CLARK

   > Christians should be happy when they embrace three truths: our bad things will turn out for good, our good things can never be taken away from us, the best things are yet to come.
   > —JONATHAN EDWARDS, PARAPHRASED FROM HIS SERMON "CHRISTIAN HAPPINESS"

   Happiness comes from seeking God—the one who created us.

2. Pick up your cross.
   - This was a revolutionary idea in Jesus' day because crosses were used by the Roman empire to execute people.

- Jesus essentially was saying, "I'm Lord, not Caesar."
- Notice: *your* cross, not *my* cross.

> Our discipleship is not just a matter of accepting Jesus' pain and sacrifice for
> us. . . . Our discipleship is also about our lives, about our own cross to bear.
>
> —MARK CLARK

> I have been crucified with Christ and I no longer live, but Christ lives in me.
> The life I now live in the body, I live by faith in the Son of God, who loved me
> and gave himself for me.
>
> —GALATIANS 2:20

- You must embrace your death—death to your desires, needs, wants, life.

> What you win people with is what you win them to.
>
> —MARK CLARK

- The Christian life is a faith of substance and obedience.

> When Christ calls a man, he bids him come and die.
>
> —DIETRICH BONHOEFFER

- Note the undercurrent of literalism when Jesus talks about death and "taking up your cross."
- Christianity is a way of life that pushes against the way of the world, and the inevitable
  clash results in pain and sometimes tragedy for the Christian.
  According to the *Oxford Christian World Encyclopedia*, throughout history there
  have been seventy-five million Christian martyrs. Forty-five million martyrs were
  killed in the twentieth century alone.

> "For whoever wants to save their life will lose it, but whoever loses their life for
> me will save it."
>
> —LUKE 9:24

- God uses our joy *and* our pain.

3. Follow me.

> The ultimate issue in the universe is leadership. Who you follow and what directs your life is the single most important thing about you.
> —JAN DAVID HETTINGA

– Christianity is about Jesus as *leader*, not just *Savior*.
– The word *disciple* occurs 269 times in the New Testament.
– The word *Christian* occurs three times in the New Testament.

> Disciple is actually the paradigm structure of Christianity.
> —MARK CLARK

– We worship a living Savior, teacher, and leader.
   Heroic story structure (Donald Miller, *Building a Storybrand*):
   • A character—the hero—has a problem.
   • They meet a guide.
   • The guide gives them a plan.
   • The plan results in action that results in either a comedy or a tragedy.
– Jesus is the hero and the guide.
– As our guide, Jesus promises freedom.

——— How Do We Follow Jesus Well? ———

• We follow with time, energy, and focus.

> This number—10,000 hours—comes up over and over again. 10,000 hours is equivalent to roughly three hours a day, or twenty hours a week of practice over ten years. No one has yet found a case in which true world-class expertise was accomplished in less time. It seems that it takes the brain this long to assimilate all that it needs to know to achieve true mastery.
> —MALCOM GLADWELL

• Jesus wanted his disciples to master a way of life and being in the world.

"Therefore go and make disciples of all nations, baptizing them in the name of the Father and of the Son and of the Holy Spirit, and teaching them to obey everything I have commanded you. And surely I am with you always, to the very end of the age."

—MATTHEW 28:19–20

• We must obey Jesus.

Vampire Christianity is when people take or receive Jesus at his cost, but not theirs (Dallas Willard). Jesus isn't interesting or compelling. You just want his blood, that's it.

From this time many of his disciples turned back and no longer followed him.

—JOHN 6:66

The call to be faithful to Jesus is a profound call.

The most important day of your marriage is the last day.

—MARK AND GRACE DRISCOLL

The Challenge:

"What do you want me to do for you?" he asked. They replied, "Let one of us sit at your right and the other at your left in your glory." "You don't know what you are asking," Jesus said. "Can you drink the cup I drink or be baptized with the baptism I am baptized with?" "We can," they answered. Jesus said to them, "You will drink the cup I drink and be baptized with the baptism I am baptized with, but to sit at my right or left is not for me to grant. These places belong to those for whom they have been prepared."

—MARK 10:36–40

——— Why Have You Chosen to Follow Jesus? ———

The adventure of Christianity is to deny yourself, pick up your cross, and follow Jesus.

Group Discussion

Take a few minutes to discuss what you just watched and explore these concepts in Scripture.

PART A

1. What stood out to you from Mark's teaching on the problem of discipleship?

   _____

   _____

   _____

   _____

   _____

2. Mark says we are all disciples ("learners") in one form or another. Let's take an honest inventory of our lives. Besides Jesus, who or what are you following and learning from?

   _____

   _____

   _____

   _____

   _____

3. **Read Matthew 4:1–11.** Also, revisit the story of the rich young ruler (Matthew 19). Mark talked about the cost of discipleship. What is the cost of discipleship for Jesus and for the young ruler in these passages? What is the cost of discipleship for us as followers of Jesus?

   _____

   _____

   _____

   _____

4. **Read Romans 8:12–28.** What does this passage say about sacrifice and perseverance as we follow Jesus? How does this inspire or encourage you as you endure challenges and temptations?

   _____

   _____

   _____

If you're doing session 3 in two parts, pause your discussion here. Take time to pray together as a group. Use the space at the end of this session to keep track of prayer requests and group updates. Otherwise, continue answering the questions for part B of your group discussion.

PART B

5. Why have you chosen to follow Jesus? How is this choice reflected in your life?

_____

_____

_____

_____

_____

6. **Read Luke 19:1–10.** How does Zacchaeus remedy his past life choices by choosing to deny himself in the present, and why was this so shocking to those around him? What sort of actions and decisions would be the equivalent to this in our modern day?

_____

_____

_____

_____

_____

7. **Read Galatians 2:14–21.** What prompts Paul to have this conversation with Cephas? How do Paul's words ring true for us today? In what ways have you struggled to put to death your old ways as you follow Jesus?

_____

_____

_____

_____

_____

8. **Read John 6:60–69.** Why do some of Jesus' disciples desert him? How can you relate to this story—how has it been hard for you to be a disciple of Jesus too? What keeps you following Jesus?

_____

_____

_____

_____

_____

Pray

Pray as a group before you close your time together. Thank God for the opportunity to be a disciple of Jesus and to experience the freedom of life in Jesus. Ask God to help you live abundantly and obediently so the good news of the gospel shines brightly in you and through you. May others be drawn to discipleship in Jesus because of the way his light radiates in your life. Use this space to keep track of prayer requests and group updates.

Between-Sessions
PERSONAL STUDY

Weekly Reflection

Before you begin the between-sessions exercises, briefly review your video notes for session 3. In the space below, write down the *most significant point* you took away from this session.

_____

_____

_____

_____

_____

_____

_____

_____

_____

_____

_____

Take some time to reflect on the material you covered during your group time by engaging in any or all of the following between-sessions exercises. These exercises follow the flow of the group experience with two exercises per each part of this session. As you read and experience the material, you may want to make a few notes in your guide. The primary goal of these between-sessions exercises is for your own spiritual growth and personal reflection, and it is not a requirement for group participation. *Note: the verses to read have most likely appeared in other areas of this session as well, but they are placed in these exercises for intentional reflection.* If you haven't done so already, read chapters 5 and 6 in *The Problem of Jesus.*

Part A

Day 1: Deny Yourself
Read: *Matthew 4:1–11; Luke 9:21–27*

Consider: Scholars paint a bleak picture when it comes to the lives of first-century Jews. They were living as exiles in their own land, discouraged, downtrodden, and pining after someone or something to follow. And their dreams were centered around an end-time (or eschatological) prophet, a messiah, who would end their suffering and pain and free them from the tyrannical rule of the Roman Empire by reestablishing God's rule. In essence, they longed for what they called the "kingdom of God" and a gospel of national prosperity for the Jewish people. So the promise of a better future played well in first-century Palestine. And then Jesus shows up and starts talking about how the way into this kingdom of God is to deny yourself. So what would motivate a person in the ancient world, or even our modern world, to take Jesus up on his vision of self-denial when it goes against everything we know about human psychology? The answers lies in this passage in Matthew about the temptations Jesus faced in the wilderness and in the stories we are told about Jesus at the beginning of his public life. Jesus rejected the temptations he experienced in the wilderness and embraced the painful path forward in the long game of obedience. The key to moving forward was self-denial.

Reflect: Take a few moments to reflect on your answers to these questions.

How does Jesus deny himself in the temptation in the wilderness?

_____

_____

_____

_____

_____

_____

Which temptation would have been hardest for you? Why?

_____

_____

_____

_____

_____

How can you practice self-denial as a way of following Jesus and honoring God? How can you put the needs or desires of others, or even Jesus himself, above your own today?

_____

_____

_____

_____

Pray: Close your time today by praying to God. Pray whatever comes to mind as you consider these passages and these questions.

Day 2: Take Up Your Cross
Read: *Matthew 16:21–28; Luke 23:26–27; Colossians 1:24–27*

Consider: It's no coincidence that Jesus' command to "deny yourselves" is followed by "take up your cross." He is telling his disciples, and therefore all of us, this is *what* we must do (*deny yourselves*) and this is *how* we must do it (*take up your cross*) to follow him. We will get to that last part in our next exercise. But for now, let's pay attention to what it means to *take up your cross*. While most of us have heard solid teaching on the idea that *taking up our cross* means carrying the heavy burdens we live with on a consistent basis, modern-day scholars say that the meaning changes when we consider the context of Jesus' day. For the first-century Jew living under Roman rule, the cross represented a tortuous death. And convicted criminals were required to carry their own heavy cross to the place of execution. So when Jesus said, "Take up your cross and follow me," what he actually meant was, "Be willing to suffer for me," and "Be willing to die a thousand deaths of self-denial for the sake of my kingdom." This carries a different weight than simply living with the burdens of life. This means we regularly, actively, and often painfully participate in practices where we deny our desires, even to the point of suffering, for the sake of Jesus and the kingdom of God.

Reflect: Take a few moments to reflect on your answers to these questions.

Why was this an important and hard instruction for the first-century Jewish audience of Jesus?

_____

_____

_____

_____

What did it mean for the apostle Paul to "take up his cross"?

_____

_____

_____

What does it look like for you to take up your cross? How does this influence or affect your daily life?

_____

_____

_____

Pray: Close your time today by praying to God. Pray whatever comes to mind as you consider these passages and these questions.

Part B

Day 3: Follow Me
Read: *Matthew 10:37–42; Mark 8:34–38; James 2:14–26*

Consider: We can't just think our way into Christianity; we need to live out our faith. This is why Jesus didn't simply give us a list of doctrines to believe. He gave us three simple instructions—*deny yourself, take up your cross, follow me*—that point to actions, behaviors, and habits required for discipleship. Jesus sets the thinking component aside here with these three instructions and leads with the very essence and *shape* of our lives. He's reminding us that our lives are molded by practices, and he is the model of those practices. If we want to live a life of meaning, a life that contributes to the greater good of humanity and the glory of God, then we must *follow him*. This is more than just a reformation of our thoughts and ideas—it's a reformation of our actions and our habits.

Reflect: Take a few moments to reflect on your answers to these questions.

What reason does Jesus give us for the call to follow him?

_____

_____

_____

According to these passages, what are the essential practices (actions, behaviors, habits) of following Jesus?

_____

_____

_____

_____

How does your life reflect these practices? Or what practices do you need to put into place as you follow Jesus?

_____

_____

_____

Pray: Close your time today by praying to God. Pray whatever comes to mind as you consider these passages and these questions.

Day 4: The Invitation to Discipleship
Read: *Matthew 28:18–20; Romans 8:18; Hebrews 12:2*

Consider: The invitation to discipleship is more than a call to give up our comforts, desires, and lives. It's about pursuing a greater reward. The greater goal of discipleship is that the joys, delights, and pleasures God has to offer us in the next life are infinitely better than those of this life. But how do we stave off our instinctual demand for immediate satisfaction? We do so by keeping Jesus as our focus. The secret to following Jesus and understanding his dedication to the glory of God is acknowledging his apocalyptic perspective. Jesus had a future in view that enabled him to face his present trials. He didn't suffer for the sake of suffering; he suffered because he knew there was something better in the end—the goodness and the glory of God. This is how Jesus had victory in the face of temptation in the wilderness and how he endured suffering in his life. And we, too, can embrace personal sacrifice, pain, and loss if we experience them in light of future joy. Jesus is our model for embracing the difficult path and the invitation of discipleship.

Reflect: Take a few moments to reflect on your answers to these questions.

Revisit the question mentioned in the group discussion introduction: What does discipleship mean to you?

_____

_____

_____

What did discipleship cost Jesus? And his followers?

_____

_____

_____

_____

What are the costs of your discipleship? And the rewards?

_____

_____

_____

Pray: Close your time today by praying to God. Pray whatever comes to mind as you consider these passages and these questions.

For Next Week: Read chapters 7 and 8 in _The Problem of Jesus_ and use the space below to write any insights or questions from your personal study that you want to discuss at the next group meeting.

_____

_____

_____

_____

_____

Journal, Reflections, and Notes

_____

_____

_____

_____

_____

_____

_____

_____

The Problem of
LOVING GOD

*Love the Lord your God with all your heart
and with all your soul and with all your mind
and with all your strength.*

—MARK 12:30

Welcome

There are moments in our lives when one single priority rises to the top. There's an accident, a diagnosis, or something in our lives catches on fire—literally or figuratively. And in those crucial moments, we're forced to reckon with the priorities that surface above everything else. Often, just one thing remains—the most important thing. Everything else seems small and insignificant in that moment. This is what was happening when Jesus told us all about the most important thing we need to know, the Greatest Commandment. A scribe asked Jesus to pick the most important of the six hundred laws in the Bible, as if to say, "Give me the one verse or the one command you're going to take with you when the fire starts." Without hesitation, Jesus answered the scribe: *love God with your whole self.* This is the key to everything according to Jesus—loving God with a love that consumes our heart, soul, mind, and strength. It's profound. It's deep. And it's life-changing in ways we never could have imagined. Contrary to what you may think, the idea of loving God is one of the most neglected ideas in modern Christianity despite being the key focus of Jesus' original teaching. That's why this is such an important session. So let's talk about what the Greatest Commandment means as we dive into the problem of loving God.

Share 💬

To kick things off, briefly discuss one of the following statements:

- Name a book about love or loving God that stands out to you. When did you read this book and why?

  —or—

- If your house caught on fire, what are the first three items you would grab and take with you?

Read 📖

Invite someone to read aloud the following passage as preparation for Mark's teaching. Listen for fresh insights as you hear the verses being read, and then briefly discuss the questions that follow.

> *Paul's Personal Requests and Final Greetings*
>
> Now about the collection for the Lord's people: Do what I told the Galatian churches to do. On the first day of every week, each one of you should set aside a sum of money in keeping with your income, saving it up, so that when I come no collections will have to be made. Then, when I arrive, I will give letters of introduction to the men you approve and send them with your gift to Jerusalem. If it seems advisable for me to go also, they will accompany me.
>
> After I go through Macedonia, I will come to you—for I will be going through Macedonia. Perhaps I will stay with you for a while, or even spend the winter, so that you can help me on my journey, wherever I go. For I do not want to see you now and make only a passing visit; I hope to spend some time with you, if the Lord permits. But I will stay on at Ephesus until Pentecost, because a great door for effective work has opened to me, and there are many who oppose me.
>
> When Timothy comes, see to it that he has nothing to fear while he is with you, for he is carrying on the work of the Lord, just as I am. No one, then, should treat him with contempt. Send him on his way in peace so that he may return to me. I am expecting him along with the brothers.
>
> Now about our brother Apollos: I strongly urged him to go to you with the brothers. He was quite unwilling to go now, but he will go when he has the opportunity.

Be on your guard; stand firm in the faith; be courageous; be strong. Do everything in love.

You know that the household of Stephanas were the first converts in Achaia, and they have devoted themselves to the service of the Lord's people. I urge you, brothers and sisters, to submit to such people and to everyone who joins in the work and labors at it. I was glad when Stephanas, Fortunatus and Achaicus arrived, because they have supplied what was lacking from you. For they refreshed my spirit and yours also. Such men deserve recognition.

The churches in the province of Asia send you greetings. Aquila and Priscilla greet you warmly in the Lord, and so does the church that meets at their house. All the brothers and sisters here send you greetings. Greet one another with a holy kiss.

I, Paul, write this greeting in my own hand.

If anyone does not love the Lord, let that person be cursed! Come, Lord!

The grace of the Lord Jesus be with you.

My love to all of you in Christ Jesus. Amen. (1 Corinthians 16)

What is one key insight that stands out to you from this passage?

_____

_____

_____

_____

What are the five specific commands Paul gives in the middle of this passage? Why do you think he gives these commands?

_____

_____

_____

_____

Consider as you listen to Mark's teaching: *What is the cost of not loving God?*

_____

_____

_____

_____

Watch ▶️

Play the video segment for session 4. As you watch, use the following outline to record any thoughts or concepts that stand out to you.

NOTES: PART A

——— The Most Important Commandment of All ———

One of the teachers of the law came and heard them debating. Noticing that Jesus had given them a good answer, he asked him, "Of all the commandments, which is the most important?"

—MARK 12:28

"The most important one," answered Jesus, "is this: 'Hear, O Israel: The Lord our God, the Lord is one. Love the Lord your God with all your heart and with all your soul and with all your mind and with all your strength.' The second is this: 'Love your neighbor as yourself.' There is no commandment greater than these."

—MARK 12:29–31

Love God as you love yourself. The most important law out of the six hundred laws of the Bible.

Book: *The True Christian's Love to the Unseen Christ* by Thomas Vincent

A common question for teachers in ancient Israel: *What is the greatest commandment?*

——— What Does It Mean to Love God? ———

A priority is something we possess at the level of heart and soul *instead of religious practice.*
Kardia is the Greek word for "heart," the center of someone's life.
Your relationship with Jesus needs to be centered around love of God.

——— What Is Scandalous about the Command to Love God? ———

We're hardwired to love, but Jesus is asking us to love God above all else.
Love of stuff over God:

For although they knew God, they neither glorified him as God nor gave thanks to him, but their thinking became futile and their foolish hearts were darkened.

—ROMANS 1:21

We exchanged the joy and love of God for the fruit—*created things*—and we loved those things instead.

We take a good thing and make it a God thing.

REPLACEMENTS FOR LOVE AND FOR GOD

- Money
- Sex
- Power
- Family
- Comfort
- Religion

Jesus replied, "Foxes have dens and birds have nests, but the Son of Man has no place to lay his head."

—LUKE 9:58

A willingness to give up comfort and ease is central to what it means to follow and love Jesus.

—MARK CLARK

Our possessions provide safety and status.

Do We Love Our Possessions More than We Love God?

The problem *isn't* our things—it's when the things become *ultimate* things.

Could You Hear God Right Now If He Called You to Something Else?

There is obedience in our complete detachment from idols.

Often being in the center of the will of God is the most dangerous place to be.

For example:

- *Paul*—2 Corinthians 11
- *Joseph*—Genesis and Exodus
- *Job*—the Book of Job
- *Jesus*—Matthew, Mark, Luke, and John

> And do not grieve the Holy Spirit of God, with whom you were sealed for the day of redemption.
>
> —EPHESIANS 4:30

Security vs. Safety

In Christ, God promises security, not safety.

- Safety promises *comfort* and *ease*.
- Security promises *God's presence* and a *future*.

Family

> Jesus said to him, "Let the dead bury their own dead, but you go and proclaim the kingdom of God."
>
> —LUKE 9:60

> Jesus replied, "No one who puts a hand to the plow and looks back is fit for service in the kingdom of God."
>
> —LUKE 9:62

The call of Jesus takes priority over our families.
This includes how you relate to your spouse.
Sometimes the people we love the most are the ones who keep us from following God.
Jump ahead to the group discussion if you're doing this session in two parts.

NOTES: PART B

——— How Do We Love God Well? ———

Saint Augustine claimed that we are what we love.
We have to *change* what we love if we want to love God well.

———— How Is It Possible to Hate the Things of the World ———— When, in Many Ways, They Are So Satisfying?

The heart is such that the only way to dispossess it of an old affection is by the expulsive power of a new one. . . .

The youth ceases to idolize pleasure, but it's only because the idol of wealth has become stronger. The love of money ceases to have mastery over the citizen because they're drawn into the world of politics. So, now they are lorded over by a love of power. The way to disengage the heart from the love of one great object is to fasten it to another. it's not about exposing the worthlessness of the old affection but exposing the worth and excellence of the new one.

—THOMAS CHALMERS

Taste and see that the LORD is good;
blessed is the one who takes refuge in him.

—PSALM 34:8

The heart needs to fasten itself to something it loves more than sin.
It's not about running away from sin—it's about running toward Jesus.

There is no other way by which to keep the love of the world out of the heart than to keep in our hearts the love of God.

—THOMAS CHALMERS

———— How Is It Possible to Come to Love God in This Way? ————

Take delight in the LORD,
and he will give you the desires of your heart.

—PSALM 37:4

The greatest gift is God himself.
We relate to God because of the benefit of his blessings.

For Christ also suffered once for sins, the righteous for the unrighteous, to bring you to God. He was put to death in the body but made alive in the Spirit.

—1 PETER 3:18

The gospel is not a way to get people to heaven; it is a way to get people to God.

—JOHN PIPER

——— Do You See and Feel the Worth of God as the End in and of Itself? ———

As the deer pants for streams of water,
> so my soul pants for you, my God.

—PSALM 42:1

Yet to all who did receive him, to those who believed in his name, he gave the right to become children of God.

—JOHN 1:12

The issue is not just welcoming the truth, but being willing to have the love of the truth in our hearts.

—JONATHAN EDWARDS

This is the verdict: Light has come into the world, but people loved darkness instead of light because their deeds were evil.

—JOHN 3:19

Love is the main thing in saving faith, the life and power of it by which it produces its great effects.

—JONATHAN EDWARDS

——— Do We Actually Love Christ? ———

If anyone does not love the Lord, let that person be cursed! Come, Lord!

—1 CORINTHIANS 16:22

Hell is for the one who is without love for Jesus. **Believing in Jesus as God is not enough. We must also love him.**

Group Discussion

Take a few minutes to discuss what you just watched and explore these concepts in Scripture.

PART A

1. What stood out to you from Mark's teaching on the problem of loving God?

    _____

    _____

    _____

    _____

    _____

2. **Read Matthew 22:34–40 and Mark 12:28–34.** What differences do you notice between the ways Matthew and Mark recorded the Greatest Commandment? Which passage resonates the most with you, and why?

    _____

    _____

    _____

    _____

    _____

3. When have you taken a "good thing" and made it a "God thing," meaning how have you elevated good things in your life above God? How do you correct your course and make things right when this happens?

    _____

    _____

    _____

    _____

    _____

4. **Read Genesis 22 and 1 Samuel 3.** How did Abraham, Eli, and Samuel respond to the voice of God? Take an honesty inventory of your life. Could you hear God if he called you to something else right now, or are your needs for safety, security, and pleasing your family drowning God's voice out?

    _____

    _____

    _____

    _____

If you're doing session 4 in two parts, pause your discussion here. Take time to pray together as a group. Use the space at the end of this session to keep track of prayer requests and group updates. Otherwise, continue answering the questions for part B of your group discussion.

PART B

5. **Read Psalm 34.** How is it possible to "turn from evil and do good" and to "hate" the things of the world when, in many ways, they are so satisfying?

_____

_____

_____

_____

_____

6. **Read Psalm 37:1–28.** According to this passage, what does it look like to love God and do good? What are the blessings of loving God in this way?

_____

_____

_____

_____

7. What kind of results come from not loving God above all else? What reasons do we give for saying we love God but not actually placing him as our top priority?

_____

_____

_____

_____

8. **Read 1 Corinthians 13.** Consider having this kind of love and expressing it to God. How does your perspective on this well-known passage change when you consider loving God in this way?

_____

_____

_____

_____

Pray

Pray as a group before you close your time together. Thank God for the opportunity to love God and be loved by God. Ask God to help you see where your priorities have been out of order and where you need to place him first in your life. Pray that others are drawn to loving God because of the way you love God. Use this space to keep track of prayer requests and group updates.

Between-Sessions
PERSONAL STUDY

Weekly Reflection

Before you begin the between-sessions exercises, briefly review your video notes for session 4. In the space below, write down the *most significant point* you took away from this session.

_____

_____

_____

_____

_____

_____

_____

_____

_____

_____

_____

Take some time to reflect on the material you covered during your group time by engaging in any or all of the following between-sessions exercises. These exercises follow the flow of the group experience with two exercises per each part of this session. As you read and experience the material, you may want to make a few notes in your guide. The primary goal of these between-sessions exercises is for your own spiritual growth and personal reflection, and it is not a requirement for group participation. *Note: the verses to read have most likely appeared in other areas of this session as well, but they are placed in these exercises for intentional reflection.* If you haven't done so already, read chapters 7 and 8 in *The Problem of Jesus.*

Part A

Day 1: The Scandal of the Greatest Commandment
Read: *Mark 12:28–34*

Consider: Human beings are hardwired to love, even if that love proves to be self-destructive. Our desires, or "loves," drive who we are and what we become. So it's not scandalous that Jesus tells us to *love*; it's scandalous that Jesus tells us what (or rather *whom*) to love. When he gives us the Greatest Commandment, it's as though Jesus raises a challenge, saying: *What do you already love with all your heart, mind, soul, and strength? Now change it. Transfer that affection to God instead. Make everything else you love secondary in your life. Leave it all behind—except for your love for God—when the house is on fire.* This is the challenge to love with the full God-given capacity with which we've been created to love; to love with the infinite kind of love that, when channeled elsewhere, is so potent that it has the power to consume us, even destroy us. This is not the sentimental, even trite, version of love we experience in our modern world today—even in our modern Christianity. This is the scandalous, deep, all-encompassing love of God.

Reflect: Take a few moments to reflect on your answers to these questions.

What did this commandment mean for the first-century Jew?

_____

_____

_____

_____

What does this commandment mean for you?

_____

_____

_____

_____

How are you loving God with your heart? Your soul? Your mind? And your strength?

_____

_____

_____

Pray: Close your time today by praying to God. Pray whatever comes to mind as you consider these passages and these questions.

Day 2: Heart and Soul
Read: *Matthew 22:36–38; Deuteronomy 6:1–9*

Consider: We know from Mark's teaching that Jesus was not the first person to be asked to name the greatest command. Historians tells us it was a common question often asked of first-century rabbis to help people decide which teacher they wanted to follow. The answer they gave cut to the heart of what the rabbi felt was most important in life. For Jesus, this was *loving God*. But what the first-century Jews were about to learn by following Jesus was that loving God meant the priority was no longer the list of external religious practices, but a change on the inside—of internal affections and desires. Of course those internal changes had outward expressions of what it meant to love God. Obedience was no longer a prerequisite of loving God, it was now the *result* of loving him. Followers of Jesus no longer needed to check boxes off their religious practices list, but they did need a change of the heart and soul. It was a paradigm shift from *belief in* God to *love for* God. This is what it meant for them to love God with all of their heart and soul. And the same is true for us today.

Reflect: Take a few moments to reflect on your answers to these questions.

Why was this a challenging mindset shift to make for the first-century Jewish audience of Jesus?

_____

_____

_____

Why does Jesus add to the original commandment found in Deuteronomy?

_____

_____

_____

How are you loving God by loving your neighbor and yourself?

_____

_____

_____

Pray: Close your time today by praying to God. Pray whatever comes to mind as you consider these passages and these questions.

Part B

Day 3: The Problem of Idols
Read: *Genesis 3; Luke 9:57–62*

Consider: When we give our whole heart, mind, soul, and strength to anything other than God, that thing becomes an idol, an object of our worship. The writer of Genesis is telling us that this is the fundamental problem with humanity, the problem beneath all of our problems. We take something finite and temporary—something God has made—and we try to make it satisfy that infinite longing in our lives. We take a good thing and make it a God thing. The finite God replacements range from the familiar bad guys—money, sex, and power—to the more insidious and hidden ones—things like our family, our comfort, or even religion itself. Again, *anything* can become a replacement for God, and sometimes the most difficult idols to identify are the very good things in our lives that keep us from fully loving God. But one of the central scandals of Jesus' ministry was how he called out the idols in people's lives. He identified the idols and called people to leave behind the things that were competing for their allegiance with God. To follow Jesus often means giving up our allegiance to anything we love more than God.

Reflect: Take a few moments to reflect on your answers to these questions.

What idols are identified in the passages you read today?

_____

_____

_____

_____

Which idols do you struggle with the most?

_____

_____

_____

_____

How can you let go of your allegiance to those idols and love God? What does this look like in a real, tangible way for you?

_____

_____

_____

_____

Pray: Close your time today by praying to God. Pray whatever comes to mind as you consider these passages and these questions.

Day 4: The Power of Love
Read: *2 Timothy 1:6–12; Ephesians 3:14–21*

Consider: Saint Augustine claimed that we are what we love. And this is true in so many ways. If our highest love is family, we will choose the good of our family over the good of other families. If it's our nation, we will choose the good of our nation over the good of all others. If our love is for our individual interests, we will serve ourselves over seeking to meet the needs of others. This is the power love has over us. Only if our highest love is *God* will we be freed up to love and serve *all* people, families, classes, and races because God's interests are paramount. God is fully and completely desirable in and of himself. He is all goodness, pure pleasure, and wholly fulfilling. In other words, we should love God because he is extremely lovable, and for no reason beyond that. He is the only thing that is an end in itself. We don't have to make our love turn God into those things, God already is those things. We simply have to turn our attention, affection, desire, and love toward God in order to experience the power of love in God. There are a hundred reasons Jesus invites us to love God with all we are, but the Greatest Commandment to love God with all our heart, soul, mind, and strength is the one that immediately changes us in profound and life-altering ways. This is the power of love.

Reflect: Take a few moments to reflect on your answers to these questions.

How have you experienced the power of love in your life?

_____

_____

_____

_____

Consider the power of God's love. What does the power of God's love look like, feel like, sound like to you?

_____

_____

_____

How do you stay connected to the power of God's love on a consistent basis?

_____

_____

_____

Pray: Close your time today by praying to God. Pray whatever comes to mind as you consider these passages and these questions.

For Next Week: Read chapters 9 and 10 in *The Problem of Jesus* and use the space below to write any insights or questions from your personal study that you want to discuss at the next group meeting.

_____

_____

_____

_____

Journal, Reflections, and Notes

_____

_____

_____

_____

_____

_____

_____

_____

The Problem of
MIRACLES

Jesus performed many other signs in the presence of his disciples, which are not recorded in this book.

—JOHN 1:30

Welcome

There are many reasons people distrust Jesus. One of the primary reasons for that distrust is his miracles. I believe it takes more faith to be skeptical about miracles than it does to believe in them. Back in Jesus' day, rationalists scrutinized his miracles, denied the plain evidence, and sought alternative explanations—such as the devil or magical powers—for them. In modern times today, we just insist miracles don't happen. Therefore, if miracles don't happen, then Jesus couldn't have done them, and the claims that he did simply are "not true." And this modern-day skepticism extends to the whole Bible. Belief in miracles is seen as something for the ancient mind (naive and uninformed) or for the mystical mind (distant and otherworldly) but not for the modern, scientific mind. And yet modern, scientific truth points to the probability of miracles given the kind of world we live in and the universe we inhabit. Contrary to popular opinion, there is actually little conflict between miracles and science. In fact, the more science delves deeper into the mysterious workings of the universe, the more miracles seem to fit. This is the problem of miracles.

Share 💬

To kick things off, briefly discuss one of the following statements:

- Name a miracle of Jesus recorded in the Gospels that stands out to you, and share why.
  —or—
- Have you ever witnessed a miracle in yours or someone else's life? If so, what was it?

Read 📖

Invite someone to read aloud the following passage as preparation for Mark's teaching. Listen for fresh insights as you hear the verses being read, and then briefly discuss the questions that follow.

Jesus Feeds the Five Thousand

The apostles gathered around Jesus and reported to him all they had done and taught. Then, because so many people were coming and going that they did not even have a chance to eat, he said to them, "Come with me by yourselves to a quiet place and get some rest."

So they went away by themselves in a boat to a solitary place. But many who saw them leaving recognized them and ran on foot from all the towns and got there ahead of them. When Jesus landed and saw a large crowd, he had compassion on them, because they were like sheep without a shepherd. So he began teaching them many things.

By this time it was late in the day, so his disciples came to him. "This is a remote place," they said, "and it's already very late. Send the people away so that they can go to the surrounding countryside and villages and buy themselves something to eat."

But he answered, "You give them something to eat."

They said to him, "That would take more than half a year's wages! Are we to go and spend that much on bread and give it to them to eat?"

"How many loaves do you have?" he asked. "Go and see."

When they found out, they said, "Five—and two fish."

Then Jesus directed them to have all the people sit down in groups on the green grass. So they sat down in groups of hundreds and fifties. Taking the five loaves and the two fish and looking up to heaven, he gave thanks and broke the loaves. Then he gave them to his disciples to distribute to the people. He also divided the two fish among them all. They all ate and were satisfied, and the disciples picked up twelve basketfuls of broken pieces of bread and fish. The number of the men who had eaten was five thousand. (Mark 6:30–44)

What is one key insight that stands out to you from this passage?

_____

_____

_____

_____

Have you ever sensed God saying to you, like Jesus said to the disciples, "Give them what you have," even when it didn't seem like enough?

_____

_____

_____

_____

Consider as you listen to Mark's teaching: *What did the miracles of Jesus mean for ancient Israel, and what do they mean for us today?*

_____

_____

_____

Watch ▶

Play the video segment for session 5. As you watch, use the following outline to record any thoughts or concepts that stand out to you.

NOTES: PART A

Key question: What do we do with stories about the supernatural?

—— The Miracles of Jesus ——

Denial and scrutiny of Jesus' miracles

Alternative explanations for his miracles:

- It's the devil.
- It's magic.
- Miracles simply don't happen because they can't happen.

> The march of science has continued to trample the belief in the supernatural.
>
> —MARK CLARK

> It takes more faith to be skeptical about miracles than it does to actually believe in them.
>
> —MARK CLARK

> Faith in miracles must yield ground, step by step, before the steady and firm advance of the forces of science, and its total defeat is indubitably a mere matter of time.
>
> —MAX PLANCK

Miracles are actually probable in our world.

Key question: Are miracles actually possible?

A *naturalist* is a person who believes that we can know everything about the world simply through the scientific evidence, experiments, and observation of the natural world.

According to naturalism, we have to approach the scientific data with a blank slate versus our prior experience.

> If anything extraordinary seems to have happened, we can always say that we or they who experienced it have been victims of illusion. If we hold a philosophy which excludes the supernatural, this is what we shall always say. What we learn from experience depends on the kind of philosophy we bring to experience.
>
> —C. S. LEWIS

If miracles are possible, even when they seem improbable, then the right evidence could convince us that miracles have actually occurred.

——— Paying Attention to the Evidence ———

> The existing evidence will be sufficient to convince us that actually quite a number of miracles have actually occurred.
>
> —C. S. LEWIS

The naturalistic approach suggests *that the world is all there is.*

• The naturalistic approach is a philosophical assumption.

> Nature is the whole show. Nothing exists or happens outside of natural realities, or what we have called the laws of nature.
>
> —C. S. LEWIS

• Scientific laws are not immutable. They are not necessarily laws of nature, they are human interpretations.

> When a thing professes from the very outset to be a unique invasion of Nature by something from the outside, increasing knowledge of Nature can never make it either more or less credible.
>
> —C. S. LEWIS

• Miracles are not contradictions of science; they lie outside the realm of science.
• Other things that also exist outside the realm of science: ethics, morality, and beauty.

Miracles interrupt the usual course of nature.

——— Biblical Miracles ———

• The act of an author injects a new element into a story, but one that rings true to the way things work already, just on a different scale.

> God creates the vine and teaches it to draw up water by its roots and, with the aid of the sun, to turn that water into a juice which will ferment and take on certain qualities. Thus every year from Noah's time till ours, God turns water into wine.
>
> —C. S. LEWIS

• The argument for miracles is an argument for an "X factor" that goes above and beyond nature—this is what makes them "supernatural."

——— The Biblical View of God ———

God is intimately involved in all things, and yet he's distinct from it—outside nature.

> That power is the same as the mighty strength he exerted when he raised Christ from the dead and seated him at his right hand in the heavenly realms.
>
> —EPHESIANS 1:19–20

> But God raised him from the dead, freeing him from the agony of death, because it was impossible for death to keep its hold on him.
>
> —ACTS 2:24

The resurrection does not contradict the laws of nature.

> Only if the atheist has independent reasons to think that God's existence is implausible or his intervention in the world is implausible could he justifiably regard the resurrection hypothesis as implausible.
>
> —WILLIAM LANE CRAIG

Religious skeptics make the mistake of defining nature as a closed system of reality. *Key question: Is there a conflict?*

——— Modern Science ———

Old science vs. new science

> Miracles actually have complete consistency with modern science. To give an example, the older modernistic way of thinking held that no event could be uncaused in any way, but if you go look up the entire field of quantum theory today, it's founded on the very notion of uncaused events.
>
> —MARK CLARK

Quantum theory

Before we decide if something has happened or not, we must consider whether or not it's actually *possible* and how *probable*.

Claims of miracles in the modern world: *200 million*

In fact, out of the millions of claims and miracle events throughout history, it would only take one of those events being true to overthrow the entire naturalistic worldview.

—CRAIG KEENER

The New Picture of the Universe

This means miracles are more probable and possible than ever.

If we try to define a miracle as an event that is incompatible with laws of nature, then it seems that water changing into wine, a dead man, coming back to life, etc., are not miracles because they're not incompatible with quantum mechanics.

—JOHN EARMAN

The universe is way more complicated than we originally thought.
The laws of nature are being rewritten all of the time.

Special divine action, including miracles, is by no means incompatible with quantum mechanics. That is because (again) quantum mechanics doesn't determine a specific outcome for a given set of initial conditions, but instead merely assigns probabilities to the possible outcomes. . . . There is no question that special divine action is consistent with science; and even the most stunning miracles are not clearly inconsistent with the laws now promulgated by science.

—ALVIN PLANTINGA

The Trouble with Probability

It is a mistake to equate evidence with probability.

If it's true that we cannot believe in one-time events that are unwitnessed and mathematically improbable, then by the same logic the naturalist can't even believe in the big bang or the idea that organic life originated through unguided evolution because we weren't around to see it. . . . So in the end, the skeptic actually fails to fully consider the evidence of rare events. Instead, they focus on the evidence for regular events and suggest that that somehow makes all rare events unworthy of belief.

—MARK CLARK

——— Rare Evidence vs. Regular Evidence ———

The evidence for the regular is not always greater than the rare.

—MARK CLARK

- Origin of the universe
- Origin of life

Had [Hume] lived in our day, an argument based on the nonexperience of miracles would have proved much more difficult and less persuasive to his contemporaries. . . . Scholars are no longer entitled to simply dismiss the possibility of supernatural causation outright for some extranormal experiences.

—CRAIG KEENER

Rarity is not the same as plausibility.
We lack complete and full knowledge of what the laws of nature are.
Jump ahead to the group discussion if you're doing this session in two parts.

NOTES: PART B

——— The Miracles of Jesus: What They Meant in His Life and Ministry ———

Key question: What do the miracles actually mean?

There's no other major religion in which miracles occur so centrally as Christianity, and no founder of any other major religion outside of Christianity who have miracles actually attributed to them in the earliest and most fundamental documents, meaning the Gospels.

—MARK CLARK

KEY QUESTIONS

Is there historical evidence that miracles were part of Jesus' life and ministry?
And if so, what did those miracles mean?

——— The Evidence of the Miracles of Jesus ———

- Thirty-one percent of Mark's gospel deals with the miracles of Jesus.
- A dozen historical documents speak of Jesus' miracles.

The church did not invent the charge that Jesus was in league with Beelzebub, but charges like that are not advanced and less they are needed as an explanation for some quite remarkable phenomenon.

—N. T. WRIGHT

- The Gospels are free from embellishment as they downplay the miracles.
- Jesus often performs miracles only in front of his disciples.
- The ministry of Jesus was quite subdued—thirty-one miracles in three years of ministry.

Jesus performed many other signs in the presence of his disciples, which are not recorded in this book.

—JOHN 1:30

The thirty-one miracles of Jesus include:

- Six exorcisms
- Seventeen healings
- Eight nature miracles

Most people sought divine help at healing sanctuaries, public individual miracle workers were not nearly so common in this period as we thought. And those who did perform wonders rarely specialized in healings.

—CRAIG KEENER

The feeding of the five thousand is the only miracle that makes it into all four of the Gospels.

Other nature miracles:

- The stilling of the storm (Mark 4)
- Turning water into wine (John 2)
- The walking on water (Matthew 14; Mark 6; John 6)

Skeptics present these as untrustworthy as they resemble earlier miracle stories:

- The stilling of the storm (Mark 4) and the Jonah story (Jonah 1–4)
- The feeding of the five thousand (Matthew 14) and the feeding of a hundred (2 Kings 4)
- Turning water into wine (John 2) and water into blood (Exodus 7)

It's more probable that Jesus crafted and performed these miracles as a way to reconstitute Israel and point back to the stories as the fulfillment of the stories.

——— The Meaning of the Miracles of Jesus ———

Common phrases used to describe Jesus' miracles:

- A *sign*—something that points to or indicates something else
- A *wonder*—an event that causes people to be amazed and astonished
- A *mighty deed or a mighty work* (a "marvel" in Greek)—an act of displaying great power, even divine power

The actions of Jesus point to deeper revelations of God and salvation to the world. Jesus' miracles always had an aim, a theological purpose.

> The Messiah was not going to save the world by miraculous, Band-Aid interventions: a storm calmed here, a crowd fed there, a mother-in-law cured back down the road. Rather, it was going to be saved by means of a deeper, darker left-handed mystery.
> —ROBERT FARRAR CAPON

The miracles are "pointers"—they relay important information about life and about the redemption of Jesus.

> But for one exception, the cursing of the fig tree, all the miracles of Jesus are redemptive. He did not come to condemn the world, but to save it.
> —HERMAN BAVINCK

The life of Jesus was always about revelation and restoration.

> Death, decay, entropy, and destruction are the true suspensions of God's laws; miracles are our early glimpses of restoration. In the words of Jürgen Moltmann, "Jesus' healings

are not supernatural miracles in a natural world. They are the only truly 'natural' things in a world that is unnatural, demonized, and wounded."

—PHILIP YANCEY

Jesus is bringing out the new creation.

> As he went along, he saw a man blind from birth. His disciples asked him, "Rabbi, who sinned, this man or his parents, that he was born blind?"
>
> —JOHN 9:1–2

> Jesus said, "For judgment I have come into this world, so that the blind will see and those who see will become blind." Some Pharisees who were with him heard him say this and asked, "What? Are we blind too?" Jesus said, "If you were blind, you would not be guilty of sin; but now that you claim you can see, your guilt remains."
>
> —JOHN 9:39–41

The disciples are looking backward to find out *why?* But Jesus points them forward to the work of God in this man's life.

The miracle made a theological point about *spiritual* blindness.

This is how miracles work: the *words* of Jesus are accompanied by the *works* of Jesus.

• Miracles are signs—of restoration to God and a new creation.

> They [miracles] not only work to show the world the redemptive plan of God, but they help us better know and understand the redemptive person of God.
>
> —MARK CLARK

• Miracles are invitations.
• Miracles are a revelation of who Jesus is and a new way of salvation.

——— What about Miracles Today? ———

> Now while he was in Jerusalem at the Passover Festival, many people saw the signs he was performing and believed in his name.
>
> —JOHN 2:23

Finally the other disciple, who had reached the tomb first, also went inside. He saw and believed.

—JOHN 20:8

He answered, "A wicked and adulterous generation asks for a sign! But none will be given it except the sign of the prophet Jonah."

—MATTHEW 12:39

These examples of rebuke are given to hostile unbelievers who see miracles and yet do not follow Jesus.

Interpretations that view miracles negatively also ignore the fact that miracles do not always lead to shallow faith. Sometimes it actually produces true and lasting faith in God.

—MARK CLARK

This salvation, which was first announced by the Lord, was confirmed to us by those who heard him. God also testified to it by signs, wonders and various miracles, and by gifts of the Holy Spirit distributed according to his will.

—HEBREWS 2:3–4

——— Miracles as Revelation of God ———

Nearby stood six stone water jars, the kind used by the Jews for ceremonial washing, each holding from twenty to thirty gallons.

—JOHN 2:6

A Jewish ritual is being fulfilled by Jesus.

The Jews then responded to him, "What sign can you show us to prove your authority to do all this?" Jesus answered them, "Destroy this temple, and I will raise it again in three days." They replied, "It has taken forty-six years to build this temple, and you are going to raise it in three days?" But the temple he had spoken of was his body.

—JOHN 2:18–21

The Jewish temple is being replaced by Jesus.

This is the problem—the scandal—of Jesus' miracles: Jesus was replacing the old way with the new way of God.

In every miracle, Jesus reinforces what he taught.

Key question: What does this have to do with us?

——— Miracles as Transformation ———

"Everyone brings out the choice wine first and then the cheaper wine after the guests have had too much to drink; but you have saved the best till now."

—JOHN 2:10

The old ways are like bad wine.

The real transformation of water into wine is about us.

It's the story that promises to take the bland ruins of our tasteless lives and make them sweet again.

—MARK CLARK

To see people transformed into fully devoted followers of Jesus.

—THE MISSION STATEMENT OF VILLAGE CHURCH

God takes us and transforms who we were into the image of Jesus, his son.

For those God foreknew he also predestined to be conformed to the image of his Son, that he might be the firstborn among many brothers and sisters.

—ROMANS 8:29

——— Does Christianity Work? ———

Transformation economy: an experience or a product that tries to transform your life.

Christianity transforms lives.

But the fruit of the Spirit is love, joy, peace, forbearance, kindness, goodness, faithfulness, gentleness and self-control. Against such things there is no law.

—GALATIANS 5:22–23

Everything changes for the better—*transforms*—with Jesus.

But transformation is painful.

The Voyage of the Dawn Treader by C. S. Lewis—Eustace "felt smaller."

Everything is part of the story God is writing in the world.

———— The Miracles of Jesus Help Us See ———— the World in a New Way

Key question: Do we want to embrace the way to that new world or not?

> "Woman, why do you involve me?" Jesus replied. "My hour has not yet come."
>
> —JOHN 2:4

> "Father, if you are willing, take this cup from me; yet not my will, but yours be done."
>
> —LUKE 22:42

> "Are not two sparrows sold for a penny? Yet not one of them will fall to the ground outside your Father's care."
>
> —MATTHEW 10:29

We *will* face trials and difficulty as we follow Jesus.

Sometimes God's answer to our prayer for a miracle is no.

There are no easy, quick answers on the road to transformation.

> When we face demons in our lives, the answer most often is not deliverance but discipleship.
>
> —MARK CLARK

Miracle stories bring us closer to God.

> At once the Spirit sent him out into the wilderness.
>
> —MARK 1:12

There are people who see the sign but don't understand it.

There are people who see the sign and believe.

Then he turned to his disciples and said privately, "Blessed are the eyes that see what you see."

—LUKE 10:23

The miracles of Jesus are about him and how good he is.

I am a poor wretch whom God took charge of, and for whom he has done so indescribably much more than I ever expected . . . that I only long for the peace of eternity in order to do nothing but thank him.

—SØREN KIERKEGAARD

Group Discussion

Take a few minutes to discuss what you just watched and explore these concepts in Scripture.

PART A

1. What stood out to you from Mark's teaching on the problem of Jesus' miracles?

_____

_____

_____

2. How do you respond to modern-day stories of the supernatural? And what does your faith community say about these stories?

_____

_____

_____

_____

3. **Read Ephesians 1.** Based on this passage, what reason does Mark give us for saying the resurrection does not contradict the laws of nature?

_____

_____

_____

4. **Read Acts 2.** What other miracles are happening in this passage as they reflect on the miracle of the resurrection? How does this passage describe Jesus replacing the "old" with the "new"?

_____

_____

_____

_____

If you're doing session 5 in two parts, pause your discussion here. Take time to pray together as a group. Use the space at the end of this session to keep track of prayer requests and group updates. Otherwise, continue answering the questions for part B of your group discussion.

PART B

5. **Read Mark 1:16–45.** Why do you think Jesus downplays his miracles and asks for people to remain quiet about them? From your perspective, when is it considered wise to stay quiet about miracles, or wise to speak up about them?

_____

_____

_____

_____

6. **Read John 2.** What else do you notice about the miracles performed here? How does this message of Jesus translate to our lives today?

_____

_____

_____

_____

7. **Read John 4:43–54.** What reason does Jesus give for performing "signs and wonders"? How is the same true for Christians and nonbelievers today?

_____

_____

_____

_____

8. **Read John 20.** The resurrection is just the start of a few miracles performed by Jesus before he ascended into heaven. What other miracles do we see in this passage, and why are they so significant to the message of the gospel today?

_____

_____

_____

_____

_____

Pray

Pray as a group before you close your time together. If you're struggling with unbelief today, ask God to help you believe in the signs and wonders of Jesus. Ask God for eyes to see and ears to hear the miracles in your everyday life. Repent of the ways you've doubted and questioned the mystery of God in Jesus. Thank God for the ways he has miraculously transformed your life and your community. Use this space to keep track of prayer requests and group updates.

_____

_____

_____

_____

_____

_____

_____

_____

_____

_____

_____

_____

_____

_____

Between-Sessions
PERSONAL STUDY

Weekly Reflection

Before you begin the between-sessions exercises, briefly review your video notes for session 5. In the space below, write down the *most significant point* you took away from this session.

_____

_____

_____

_____

_____

_____

_____

_____

_____

_____

_____

_____

Take some time to reflect on the material you covered during your group time by engaging in any or all of the following between-sessions exercises. These exercises follow the flow of the group experience with two exercises per each part of this session. As you read and experience the material, you may want to make a few notes in your guide. The primary goal of these between-sessions exercises is for your own spiritual growth and personal reflection, and it is not a requirement for group participation. *Note: the verses to read have most likely appeared in other areas of this session as well, but they are placed in these exercises for intentional reflection.* If you haven't done so already, read chapters 9 and 10 in *The Problem of Jesus*.

Part A

Consider: The idea that miracles are not possible comes from the worldview of *naturalism*. This is the idea that nature is the "whole show"—a total system in which everything can be explained by hypothesis, observation, and experiment, and nothing exists or happens outside of natural realities or the "laws of nature." In naturalism, there is not spiritual or immaterial world, only a material world we can test, see, feel, touch, and smell. This might sound reasonable, and yet the argument of naturalism has proven faulty when challenged and as credible contradictions begin to emerge from it. For instance, it's a contradiction to say that scientific laws are "immutable" laws of nature when they are actually human laws containing interpretations that represent our best guess about the world and the way it works. In another instance, we find that scientists and skeptics "stack the deck" and deny miracles based on their own experience or lack-there-of. This is a contradictory, circular argument and a self-fulfilling prophecy. How can you explore the idea of miracles if you claim to not have experienced miracles? Belief in naturalism, for many, denies the probability that miracles might actually happen. But miracles interrupt the usual course of nature. Think of it like catching an apple as it falls from a tree. The law of gravity isn't any less real or effective just because someone's hand got in the way. Interruptions are not contradictions, they are merely just that—interruptions. Miracles are not contradictions of nature; rather, we believe that nature cannot produce these effects when left alone. Miracles happen when something (or someone) outside the natural world intervenes.

Reflect: Take a few moments to reflect on your answers to these questions.

Have you heard the argument of naturalism vs. miracles before? If so, where and how did you respond?

_____

_____

_____

What questions do you have about the probability of miracles? Who can you talk to about these questions?

_____

_____

_____

Even if you have questions, do you still believe miracles can happen? Why or why not?

_____

_____

_____

_____

Pray: Close your time today by praying to God. Pray whatever comes to mind as you consider these passages and these questions.

> **Day 2:** The Reality of Miracles
> **Read:** *Psalm 145:4–6; Romans 1:19–21; 11:23–25*

Consider: In the biblical accounts of miracles, we find that the moment a miracle enters reality, it starts obeying all the laws of the world. There is a predictable pattern that these new events fold into. Wine will still intoxicate even when it appears by a miracle. Bread will still be eaten and digested even when it appears as a miracle. Conception still leads to pregnancy even when it begins as a miracle. The biblical view of miracles is that God is intimately involved and engaged in the miraculous details and interruptions of our lives. It's the view that God acts within the natural system in whatever way he desires at a given time. Saying that God raised Jesus from the dead does not contradict the laws of nature because God is interrupting the laws of nature for the miracle—that's what's miraculous. In other words, according to nature, a general resurrection from the dead can't actually happen. But Christianity doesn't argue this will happen according to nature; it speaks to God and his supernatural power to intervene and do something beyond the natural. A closed system of nature does not define the entirety of reality. When a miracle happens, it's not "abnormal" in the sense that it's a violation of nature, but only in the sense that it is a rare occurrence.

Reflect: Take a few moments to reflect on your answers to these questions.

How have you experienced the reality of miracles?

_____

_____

_____

How does it make you feel or what does it mean to you to consider miracles as God's intimate participation in our lives?

_____

_____

_____

How have you felt God's presence through something miraculous that has happened in your life?

_____

_____

_____

Pray: Close your time today by praying to God. Pray whatever comes to mind as you consider these passages and these questions.

Part B

Day 3: The Miracles of Jesus
Read: *Matthew 8:1–4; 12:14; Mark 1:40–44; 3:6*

Consider: There is little doubt that the Gospels and the historians at the time of Jesus claim that miracles were a part of Jesus' ministry. There were more than a dozen non-Christian references to Jesus and specific mentions of his miracles from Jewish, Greek, and Roman sources of the time. Most notable of the historians' claims are those of Josephus, a Jewish historian working for the Roman Empire during the first century. Turning to the Gospels, 31 percent of the material in Mark deals directly or indirectly with miracles. The stories of miracles in the Gospels are somewhat short and to the point, without a lot of unnecessary information or extrapolation. In this, they are quite different from other legends and myths of the time, which were prone to embellishments. But the miracle stories of Jesus are free from such embellishments. In fact, the miracles of Jesus were a problematic and controversial phenomenon for his enemies *and* his friends—and the leaders of his day plotted to kill him because of them. So why were they included in the Gospels? If the early church wanted to "whitewash" Jesus and make him more acceptable, why did they include the miracle stories in their writings? The gospel writers could have easily either excluded the stories or exaggerated them to make them more acceptable, but instead they stuck to plainly stating the details—including names and eyewitnesses—of thirty of the miracles of Jesus, while alluding to the fact that he healed many more people than they recorded. Jesus performed miracles to bring healing and wholeness while also challenging the religious laws of the day in his attempt to redefine covenant participation for all who believed in God. They were about the redemption of a broken world and broken people.

Reflect: Take a few moments to reflect on your answers to these questions.

With so much historical evidence for the miracles of Jesus, why do some still doubt them?

_____

_____

_____

If you were one of the gospel writers, how would you have been tempted to embellish or exclude the miracle stories, and why?

_____

_____

_____

Based on what we know about the miracles Jesus did perform, what do you imagine the miracles to be that were excluded from the Gospels?

_____

_____

_____

Pray: Close your time today by praying to God. Pray whatever comes to mind as you consider these passages and these questions.

Day 4: Modern-Day Miracles
Read: *John 2:23–25; 20:8; 29:31; Hebrews 2:3–4*

Consider: Jesus did miracles to reveal to the world what he came to do. He was not just healing people or doing marvelous things for the sake of doing them. In every miracle, Jesus was reinforcing what he taught—that he was replacing the temple with his body, and he was replacing the law with faith. With Jesus came a cosmic shift in how God related to the world for Jesus was bringing creation back to what it was intended to be prior to sin and death. Because of this, the miracles of Jesus were about transformation—*our* transformation. Thinking back to the first miracle of turning water into wine, Jesus came to save and transform and free people from normal, everyday, stale, water-in-a-pot existences to something sweet and colorful, something that affects the senses and stimulates the soul. The real transformation of water into wine is about *us*. It is the story that promises to take the bland scraps of our tasteless lives and make them sweet again. In this way, Jesus is still doing miracles. He transforms us from the selfish, idol-driven, sinful, hopeless people into something entirely different. And this changes our lives. *Jesus* changes us. The miracles of Jesus are an *invitation* to all of us. They are God's invitation to enter in and experience restoration at a personal level in our hearts and souls. Restoration and transformation are our modern-day miracles.

Reflect: Take a few moments to reflect on your answers to these questions.

How have you experienced transformation and restoration in Jesus?

_____

_____

_____

_____

_____

Have you considered the transformation in your life to be a miracle? If not, how does thinking about your transformation as a miracle change your perspective?

_____

_____

_____

_____

What modern-day miracle are you asking God to do?

_____

_____

_____

_____

Pray: Close your time today by praying to God. Pray whatever comes to mind as you consider these passages and these questions.

For Next Week: Read chapters 11 and 12 in *The Problem of Jesus* and use the space below to write any insights or questions from your personal study that you want to discuss at the next group meeting.

_____

_____

_____

_____

_____

Journal, Reflections, and Notes

_____

_____

_____

_____

_____

_____

_____

_____

_____

_____

_____

_____

_____

_____

_____

_____

_____

_____

_____

_____

_____

_____

The Problem of
JESUS' STORIES

*But while he was still a long way off, his father
saw him and was filled with compassion for him.*

—LUKE 15:20

Welcome

One of the central ways that we make sense of the world is by telling stories. This is how we answer the core questions we have as human beings about ourselves, others, and the world around us. Stories are our explanation of reality. They are the filter through which we experience and understand life—who we are, where we are, why we exist, how we solve our problems, and so on. Stories are how we express our worldview. But what if I told you that there were only *seven stories* for all of humankind? That *every single story* falls into one of seven categories. Surreal, right? What's even more surreal is that we just keep telling these seven stories over and over again. The same basic archetypal themes are woven throughout every story we've told for five thousand years. Stories are how we're wired; they're programmed into us. They are how we make sense of the world, and they connect us in profound ways to patterns of human psychology and our deep longings to frame the world and define how we live. Stories give meaning to our lives. This is why stories are so central to the life and teachings of Jesus. But Jesus didn't just use stories to make our lives more meaningful. Jesus told stories to challenge the status quo and demand a response that summoned his listeners to a new and better way to be human as he pointed to the kingdom of God. This was the problem of Jesus' stories.

Share

To kick things off, briefly discuss one of the following statements:

- Besides the story of Jesus, name another story you consider to be the greatest story of all time. What do you love about that story?

  —*or*—

- Which teaching parable of Jesus means the most to you, and why?

Read

Invite someone to read aloud the following passage as preparation for Mark's teaching. Listen for fresh insights as you hear the verses being read, and then briefly discuss the questions that follow.

The Parable of the Lost Son

Jesus continued: "There was a man who had two sons. The younger one said to his father, 'Father, give me my share of the estate.' So he divided his property between them.

"Not long after that, the younger son got together all he had, set off for a distant country and there squandered his wealth in wild living. After he had spent everything, there was a severe famine in that whole country, and he began to be in need. So he went and hired himself out to a citizen of that country, who sent him to his fields to feed pigs. He longed to fill his stomach with the pods that the pigs were eating, but no one gave him anything.

"When he came to his senses, he said, 'How many of my father's hired servants have food to spare, and here I am starving to death! I will set out and go back to my father and say to him: Father, I have sinned against heaven and against you. I am no longer worthy to be called your son; make me like one of your hired servants.' So he got up and went to his father.

"But while he was still a long way off, his father saw him and was filled with compassion for him; he ran to his son, threw his arms around him and kissed him.

"The son said to him, 'Father, I have sinned against heaven and against you. I am no longer worthy to be called your son.'

"But the father said to his servants, 'Quick! Bring the best robe and put it on him. Put a ring on his finger and sandals on his feet. Bring the fattened calf and kill it. Let's have a feast and celebrate. For this son of mine was dead and is alive again; he was lost and is found.' So they began to celebrate.

"Meanwhile, the older son was in the field. When he came near the house, he heard music and dancing. So he called one of the servants and asked him what was going on. 'Your brother has come,' he replied, 'and your father has killed the fattened calf because he has him back safe and sound.'

"The older brother became angry and refused to go in. So his father went out and pleaded with him. But he answered his father, 'Look! All these years I've been slaving for you and never disobeyed your orders. Yet you never gave me even a young goat so I could celebrate with my friends. But when this son of yours who has squandered your property with prostitutes comes home, you kill the fattened calf for him!'

"'My son,' the father said, 'you are always with me, and everything I have is yours. But we had to celebrate and be glad, because this brother of yours was dead and is alive again; he was lost and is found.'" (Luke 15:11–32)

What is one key insight that stands out to you from this passage?

_____

_____

_____

_____

What character do you most identify with, and why—the lost son, the older son, or the father?

_____

_____

_____

_____

Consider as you listen to Mark's teaching: *Why did Jesus teach in parables so often?*

_____

_____

_____

_____

Watch

Play the video segment for session 6. As you watch, use the following outline to record any thoughts or concepts that stand out to you.

NOTES: PART A

——— Storytelling ———

It's how we answer life's most important questions:

- *Who are we?*
- *Where are we?*
- *What's the problem?*
- *What's the solution?*

Stories are an explanation of reality.

> Narrative is the most characteristic expression of worldview, going deeper than observation or fragmented remark.
>
> —N. T. WRIGHT

Stories shape what we think about the world and how we experience it.
Book: *The Seven Basic Plots* by Christopher Booker

The Seven Stories of Humankind

1. Overcoming the monster
2. Rags to riches
3. The quest
4. Voyage and return
5. Comedy
6. Tragedy
7. The rebirth

These are the basic archetypal themes of stories for thousands of years.

So deep and instinctive is our need for those stories that, as small children, we have no sooner learned to speak then we begin demanding to be told stories. . . .

Yet what is astonishing is how incurious we are as to why we indulge in this strange form of activity. What real purpose does it serve? So much do we take our need to tell stories for granted that such questions scarcely even occur to us.

—CHRISTOPHER BOOKER

——— Jesus Was a Storyteller ———

One-third of his recorded teaching ministry in the Gospels is Jesus telling stories, or *parables.*

Teacher is the most common title used for Jesus in the Jesus tradition—occurring nearly fifty times.

—JAMES D. G. DUNN

Key questions: Why did Jesus tell stories? What was his aim?
The stories of Jesus:

- Answered the deep questions we have as humans—they frame how we see ourselves, the world, and God
- Challenged our perspectives
- Replaced our worldviews

What a mistake to think that it's the task of theology to unravel God's mystery, to bring it down to the flat, ordinary human wisdom of experience and reason! It is the task of theology solely to preserve God's wonder, to understand, to defend, to glorify God's mystery as mystery.

—DIETRICH BONHOEFFER

Jesus sought to retain the mystery and beauty of God's kingdom through his stories. Jesus used parables to free people by *freeing the imagination* of people. (Brian Walsh)

To my dear Lucy, I wrote this story for you. But when I began it, I had not realized that girls grow quicker than books. As a result, you're already too old for fairytales. And by the time it's printed and bound, you'll be older still. But someday, you'll be old enough to start reading fairytales again.

—C. S. LEWIS, DEDICATION OF *THE LION, THE WITCH AND THE WARDROBE*

Jesus gets beneath the *reasons* to the *passions* and *desires*.

Key question: Will you let the stories of Jesus derail and upend your life in order to give you meaning and purpose?

There are many stories which are shaped by more than one basic plot at a time. There are even very small number of stories, including *The Lord of the Rings*, which include all seven plots.

—CHRISTOPHER BOOKER

The Parable of the Prodigal Son (Luke 15)

What is the meaning of this story?

- The two sons are lost in different ways.
- It's not what we can do for God but what he can do for us.
- There is a celebration, grace, and generosity.
- They get a gift, not a reward.

It's a great picture of the gospel.

Jump ahead to the group discussion if you're doing this session in two parts.

NOTES: PART B

The Parable of the Prodigal Son (continued)

We are *all* lost and in need of saving.

The plight of the modern man: a sinner with no word for it or, worse, who looks up the word for it in dictionary of psychology and thus only aggravates the problem of his separateness, because all the analysis in the world doesn't allow the person to find out who he is and why he has to die. That it is when psychology, rather than theology, pretends to do this, that it becomes a fraud and an impasse from which man cannot escape.

—ERNEST BECKER

Our modern impulse is to deny our brokenness, but this crushes us under expectation.
Key question: Who are you when no one is looking?
The book *Everybody Lies* by Seth Stephens-Davidowitz is based on the idea that what we say about ourselves is vastly different than who or what we are in reality.

> The algorithms know you better than you know yourself.
> —SETH STEPHENS-DAVIDOWITZ

——— We Are Lost and We Need to Be Found ———

There are two ways to be lost:

- As the younger brother—the *unrighteous* person
- As the older brother and son—the *righteous* person

Key question: Which kind of lost person are you?

The Younger Son

You are lost, but you're also called a "son."
We are all made in the image of God.

> The highest good in the world is individual freedom, happiness, self-definition, and self-expression. . . . The primary social ethic is tolerance of everyone's self-defined quest for individual freedom and self-expression.
> —MARK SAYERS

Jesus says the opposite: *we must deny selfishness and our desire to be our own master.*
But we want to do our own thing.
We are not free when we are controlled by external circumstances.
The younger son finds freedom in relating to the father, not to himself.
Running our own lives by our own authority—this is self-inflicted slavery.
Jesus says we are lost, but he invites us into something better: *salvation and joy in God.*

The Older Son

He's lost because of religion—he has trusted in spiritual rules and regulations.

We can never *earn* our way into the kingdom of God.

> In the last day, when the books are opened, we're going to have two options before God. The first option will be to ask God to judge us on the life we lived. The second option will be to ask God to judge us based on the life Jesus lived for us. I shall take the second option. I find no hope in the first.
>
> —DARYLL JOHNSON

The story of the woman caught in adultery:

> "Let any one of you who is without sin be the first to throw a stone at her."
>
> —JOHN 8:7

> Jesus straightened up and asked her, "Woman, where are they? Has no one condemned you?"
>
> "No one, sir," she said.
>
> "Then neither do I condemn you," Jesus declared. "Go now and leave your life of sin."
>
> —JOHN 8:10–11

The order of Jesus' words matter.

Jesus saves us from our slavery and from being lost.

The "older son/brother" way of relating to the world creates *pride* rather than *humility*.

Key question: Do we know what kind of "lost-ness" we have?

——— The Father ———

He gives his sons the gift of grace.

He ran to his lost younger son.

He's extravagant in his love.

The beauty of this story is that the father has compassion and grace for *both* sons.

Key question: How will you respond to God the Father?

> Nothing in my hand I bring, simply to the cross I cling.
>
> —AUGUSTUS M. TOPLADY, "ROCK OF AGES"

Jesus used parables to create a scandal—*a crisis of faith in every listener*—to demand a response.

Key question: If the view you've held is wrong, are you brave enough to change your mind?

Group Discussion

Take a few minutes to discuss what you just watched and explore these concepts in Scripture.

PART A

1. What stood out to you from Mark's teaching on the problem of Jesus' stories?

_____

_____

_____

_____

2. Go back to your favorite story you shared in the introduction of this session. How many of the seven plots are included in your favorite story?

_____

_____

_____

_____

3. **Read Matthew 13:10–17.** What reason does Jesus give the disciples for speaking in parables?

_____

_____

_____

_____

4. **Read the parables in Matthew 13.** From your personal perspective, which parable of Jesus does the best job at "maintaining the mystery and beauty of God" or "freeing the imagination" of people?

_____

_____

_____

If you're doing session 6 in two parts, pause your discussion here. Take time to pray together as a group. Use the space at the end of this session to keep track of prayer requests and group updates. Otherwise, continue answering the questions for part B of your group discussion.

PART B

5. Now that you've had more time to consider this story, which character do you identify with the most in the parable of the lost son: the younger brother, the older brother, or the father? Why?

_____

_____

_____

_____

6. What words would you use to describe yourself when no one else is looking? Are these words similar or vastly different from the words that describe you when you're with others? If so, why do you think there's such a difference?

_____

_____

_____

_____

7. **Read John 8.** What else do you notice about the way Jesus responds to the woman in this story? How does this story influence the way you view Jesus and the way you view yourself?

_____

_____

_____

_____

8. **Read Luke 15.** According to these parables, what happens when lost things are found? What lostness are you experiencing right now, and how do you need to be saved, rescued, or found by Jesus?

_____

_____

_____

Pray

Pray as a group before you close your time together. Ask God to help you see where you are lost and need to be saved, rescued, or found. Repent of the ways you've lived according to your own authority. Thank God for the gift of Jesus' parables and the commonality we find in his stories of shared humanity. Use this space to keep track of prayer requests and group updates.

Between-Sessions
PERSONAL STUDY

Weekly Reflection

Before you begin the between-sessions exercises, briefly review your video notes for session 6. In the space below, write down the *most significant point* you took away from this session.

_____

_____

_____

_____

_____

_____

_____

_____

_____

_____

Take some time to reflect on the material you covered during your group time by engaging in any or all of the following between-sessions exercises. These exercises follow the flow of the group experience with two exercises per each part of this session. As you read and experience the material, you may want to make a few notes in your guide. The primary goal of these between-sessions exercises is for your own spiritual growth and personal reflection, and it is not a requirement for group participation. *Note: the verses to read have most likely appeared in other areas of this session as well, but they are placed in these exercises for intentional reflection.* If you haven't done so already, read chapters 11 and 12 in *The Problem of Jesus*.

Part A

Day 1: The Purpose of the Parables
Read: *Matthew 13:9–11; 21:44–26; Mark 4:10–12*

Consider: Historical Jesus research acknowledges that the most obvious category for Jesus was that of "teacher," most notably because of his use of stories to teach and illustrate the truth. One scholar points out that the only other, and possibly more accurate, title for Jesus would have been *mosel*, meaning "parabolist," or one who characteristically spoke in parables. In other words, stories were the vehicle Jesus used to communicate information in an aesthetic manner for the purpose of bringing about a new reality. He wanted to communicate in a way that went deeper and further than a simple explanation of facts. Why flatten a reality that cannot be fully captured in words without an attempt to retain the beauty and the mystery?

Reflect: Take a few moments to reflect on your answers to these questions.

How do the parables of Jesus set him apart from the other teachers, scholars, and scribes of his day?

_____

_____

_____

_____

From your perspective, which parables of Jesus capture the beauty and mystery of the gospel?

_____

_____

_____

_____

Which parable has had the greatest impact on you? Why?

_____

_____

_____

_____

Pray: Close your time today by praying to God. Pray whatever comes to mind as you consider these passages and these questions.

Day 2: Freeing the Imagination
Read: *Proverbs 1:5–7; Hosea 12:9–10; Matthew 13:34–36*

Consider: Jesus told parables to free people by first doing what is necessary: *freeing their imagination.* J. R. R. Tolkien once challenged his dear friend and fellow Oxford University professor C. S. Lewis, telling Lewis that his failure to understand God didn't lay in rational thinking but in the imagination. According to Tolkien, it was a failure that Lewis had yet to grasp the significance of God with his *imagination.* And he reminded Lewis that "myth" and "truth" are not all that far removed from one another. Many of us have benefitted from Tolkien's challenge to Lewis on this matter with our consumption of *The Chronicles of Narnia.* While Jesus sometimes chose to speak the truth plainly, more often than not he sought to retain the mystery and beauty of God's kingdom through the use of stories. He captured the imagination of people—and the entire world—with an alternative reality, something altogether different than what was offered by the kingdoms of the world.

Reflect: Take a few moments to reflect on your answers to these questions.

In what specific ways did Jesus capture the attention of his audience by speaking in parables?

_____

_____

_____

How has Jesus captured your attention through the truth and mystery of his parables?

_____

_____

_____

What other mythical stories, in print or media, have captured your attention as they seem to represent the truth and themes of the gospel?

_____

_____

_____

Pray: Close your time today by praying to God. Pray whatever comes to mind as you consider these passages and these questions.

Part B

Day 3: A Familiar Tune
Read: *Psalm 25:4–6; Matthew 22:15–22; John 1:16–18*

Consider: The parables of Jesus did far more than teach; they subverted and reimagined life, calling people to the life God intended. But this new life had a familiar ring to it for some in Jesus' audience. In fact, Jesus told stories because if his audience had ears to truly hear what he was saying, their "old souls" would hear a call from a land they had not visited but somehow knew. It was as if Jesus were singing the words to a song they hadn't heard but could somehow hum. Jesus was uniquely able to make a powerful point with his stories that had the ability to get beneath the reason of his skeptics and his audience to their passions and desires. He took the messages of ancient Israel and revealed something new in them. This made his stories feel anything but safe for him and his audience. Jesus didn't hide the message of the kingdom of God, as some people claim, rather he told the truth in riddles. Author Chaim Potok claims that telling the truth is like facing a charging bull: "People can't take the truth if it comes charging at them like a bull. The bull always gets killed." Potok was a firm believer, as well as a literary practitioner, in the idea that the truth had to be hidden in riddles so it could be found piece by piece—"that way they learn to live with it."

Reflect: Take a few moments to reflect on your answers to these questions.

How do you think Jesus' audience would have responded if he showed up on the scene and told the plain truth as an infant, an adolescent, or at the start of his public ministry?

_____

_____

_____

Notice your own response to people who are quick to confront others with the truth vs. people who use stories to illustrate what they believe to be true. How do you respond to these two?

_____

_____

_____

Which kind of person are you, and why?

_____

_____

_____

Pray: Close your time today by praying to God. Pray whatever comes to mind as you consider these passages and these questions.

> **Day 4:** Lost and Found
> **Read:** *Luke 15*

Consider: We are far more lost than we project to the world or will admit to those around us. Evidence of this is the amount of lying we do. If we're being honest, we lie to everybody all the time, even to ourselves. But we either dismiss and deny this truth, or we think we can "make it right" in our own way. Such is the burden of religion which tells us that we either don't need saving or that we are our own saviors. Jesus challenges both of these ancient and modern-day impulses by reminding us that we're made in the image of God, yet we are lost and disconnected from God. And because of this, we need saving, we need to be found. We are broken and need to be put back together again. The parable that gets to the heart of the ways we deceive ourselves is the parable of the lost son. As Luke explains, there were two groups listening to this story as Jesus told it: "tax collectors and sinners" and "Pharisees and the teachers of the law." Jesus' story about the two brothers and their father deconstructs the traditional thinking that concludes that the first group is the lost group while the second group is found. Jesus scandalously says that both groups are lost, but for opposite reasons. The two brothers are the archetypes of the two groups and, by extension, for all of humanity. Jesus' message is that one brother is lost because he is far from God, and the other brother is lost because he clings to the traditions of God rather than to God himself.

Reflect: Take a few moments to reflect on your answers to these questions.

Do you ever consider yourself lost and in need of being found? Lost in which way—far from God or clinging to religious practices instead of God himself?

_____

_____

_____

According to this parable, how do we find our way back to God once we recognize our need to be found?

_____

_____

_____

How does the father in this story represent the hopeful anticipation and merciful response of God in our own lives?

_____

_____

_____

Pray: Close your time today by praying to God. Pray whatever comes to mind as you consider these passages and these questions.

For Next Week: Read chapters 13 and 14 in *The Problem of Jesus* and use the space below to write any insights or questions from your personal study that you want to discuss at the next group meeting.

_____

_____

_____

_____

Journal, Reflections, and Notes

_____

_____

_____

_____

_____

_____

_____

_____

_____

The Problem of Jesus as God—
OR GOD AS JESUS

The Word became flesh and moved into the neighborhood.

—JOHN 1:14 MSG

Welcome

One of the most controversial aspects to any explanation of Jesus is the claim of Jesus' divinity. In our Christian worldview, we believe God himself entered our world. He didn't keep his distance and give us instructions on how to get to him. He came down the mountain and into the village to see us. God became human. He entered our *mess* through Jesus. And yet the question of Jesus' divinity is questioned and challenged by both secular and religious thinkers. On the religious side of the coin is the argument that Jesus was just an enlightened teacher—one of many spiritual gurus of history, and part of the "divine" just as we are all part of it. And on the secular side is the idea that Jesus should primarily be understood as a Jewish revolutionary who failed to achieve his goals. The issue for these thinkers has never been whether Jesus existed—there is no doubt in their minds that he did. Instead, they question his divinity and deny he was God or that he ever claimed to be God. Their desire is to show him as a man rooted in history, not "mythology." The question of Jesus' divinity is certainly one of the most definitive and dangerous ideas we will explore among the problems associated with Jesus. The problem of Jesus as God—or God as Jesus—is the ultimate scandal of the Christian faith. So let's look at the evidence.

Share 💬

To kick things off, briefly discuss one of the following statements:

- Name a metaphor commonly used by Jesus to describe himself as God in the Gospels that resonates most with you (i.e. the vine, light, word, shepherd).

  —*or*—

- Have you or someone you know ever doubted that Jesus was God? What was the reasoning?   .

Read 📖

Invite someone to read aloud the following passage as preparation for Mark's teaching. Listen for fresh insights as you hear the verses being read, and then briefly discuss the questions that follow.

> *The Word Became Flesh*
>
> In the beginning was the Word, and the Word was with God, and the Word was God. He was in the beginning with God; all things were made through him, and without him was not anything made that was made. In him was life, and the life was the light of men. The light shines in the darkness, and the darkness has not overcome it.
>
> There was a man sent from God, whose name was John. He came for testimony, to bear witness to the light, that all might believe through him. He was not the light, but came to bear witness to the light.
>
> The true light that enlightens every man was coming into the world. He was in the world, and the world was made through him, yet the world knew him not. He came to his own home, and his own people received him not. But to all who received him, who believed in his name, he gave power to become children of God; who were born, not of blood nor of the will of the flesh nor of the will of man, but of God.
>
> And the Word became flesh and dwelt among us, full of grace and truth; we have beheld his glory, glory as of the only Son from the Father.
>
> (John bore witness to him, and cried, "This was he of whom I said, 'He who comes after me ranks before me, for he was before me.'") And from his fulness have we all received, grace upon grace. For the law was given through Moses; grace and truth came through Jesus Christ. No one has ever seen God; the only Son, who is in the bosom of the Father, he has made him known. (John 1:1–18 RSV)

What is one key insight that stands out to you from this passage?

_____

_____

_____

Why does Jesus say his own people did not receive him?

_____

_____

_____

Consider as you listen to Mark's teaching: *How is the claim of Jesus as God reflected in our lives as grace and truth?*

_____

_____

Watch ▶

Play the video segment for session 7. As you watch, use the following outline to record any thoughts or concepts that stand out to you.

NOTES: PART A

——— God Himself Entered Our World ———

The Word became flesh and blood,
    and moved into the neighborhood.
We saw the glory with our own eyes,
    the one-of-a-kind glory,
    like Father, like Son,
Generous inside and out,
    true from start to finish.

—JOHN 1:14 MSG

And the Word became flesh and dwelt among us, full of grace and truth; we have beheld his glory, glory as of the only Son from the Father.

—JOHN 1:14 RSV

——— The Divinity of Jesus ———

The New Age argument for both religious and secular groups is that *Jesus was an enlightened teacher.*

Key question: Was Jesus really God?

> The supreme mystery with which the Gospel confronts us lies not in the Good Friday message of atonement, nor in the Easter message of resurrection, but in the Christmas message of Incarnation. The really staggering Christian claim is that Jesus of Nazareth was God made man.
>
> —J. I. PACKER

——— Jesus as God in the Early Church ———

> For God was pleased to have all his fullness dwell in him.
> —COLOSSIANS 1:19

> For in Christ all the fullness of the Deity lives in bodily form.
> —COLOSSIANS 2:9

> [Jesus] who, though he was in the form of God, did not count equality with God a thing to be grasped.
> —PHILIPPIANS 2:6 RSV

> But in these last days he has spoken to us by a Son, whom he appointed the heir of all things, through whom also he created the world. He reflects the glory of God and bears the very stamp of his nature, upholding the universe by his word of power.
> —HEBREWS 1:2–3 RSV

Monotheism: there is only *one* God.

> In truth, there is no doubt that, in the usage of the New Testament, the title "Lord" is regarded as the title used of God in the Old Testament, and now applied to Jesus. Most scholars actually recognize the clear passages affirming Jesus' divinity as early creeds and actual hymns that the church sang. And they confirmed what they believed as they gathered.
> —MARK CLARK

The early church worshiped Jesus as God (Philippians 2:5–11).

- Jesus is fully human *and* fully divine.
- This is not a *heresy* as claimed by Judaism and Islam.
- This is not an *impossibility* as claimed by Greek and modern thought.

———— Jesus as God in the Gospels ————

Jesus repeatedly claimed to be God, and his early followers claimed this to be true too.
Key question: Why do you believe Jesus is God when he never said it as such?

Jesus made his claim to be God through words and methods that made sense to his first-century audience.

What Jesus Said

- He invented the Sabbath and had the authority to update the rules about observing it (Mark 2).
- His knowledge was on par with God's knowledge (Matthew 11).
- He was equal with God (John 5).
- He claimed that whoever sees him, sees the Father (John 14).
- He doesn't correct the people who treat him as if he is God (Matthew 26).
- He claimed to have preexistence (John 3).
- He says he's older than Abraham (John 8).
- He replaces the temple (John 2).
- He shared glory with God before the world existed (John 17).
- He claimed thirty-nine times to be a missionary from heaven (the Gospel of John).
- He said he would send his angels (Matthew 13).
- He had the authority to forgive sins (Mark 2).
- He assumed the authority to judge the world (Mark 14:62).
- He claimed peoples' attitude towards him would define their judgement (Matthew 10).
- He was perfectly sinless (John 8).
- He had the power to raise himself from the dead (John 2).
- He claimed that to know him was to know God (John 8).
- He claimed to see him was to see God (John 12).
- He claimed to receive him was to receive God (Mark 9).
- He took on the name *I am* (Exodus 3; John 8:58).

- He claimed to be the only way to heaven (John 14).
- He said he was one with the Father (John 10).

What Jesus Did

- He taught people to pray to him (John 14)—and then we see Steven (Acts 7), Paul (1 Corinthians 1), and John (Revelation 22) praying to Jesus.
- He performs nature miracles throughout the Gospels.

> And the men marveled, saying, "What sort of man is this, that even winds and sea obey him?"
>
> —MATTHEW 8:27 RSV

- He claimed titles that were used for God in the Old Testament: Yahweh, the Shepherd of Israel, the Alpha and Omega, the Almighty, Light, First and Last, the Judge of all nations, and the Bridegroom.
- He is called Immanuel, which means "God with us" (Matthew 1).
- He didn't correct Thomas when he made a declaration of Jesus' divinity (John 20).
- He demonstrated he had the power to destroy death (John 11).
- He had the authority to forgive sins (Mark 2:7–10).
- He was the means by which Yahweh was returning to Zion (Luke 19).
- He could determine people's eternal destiny before God (Luke 12).

Jesus claimed to be God through both word and deed in a culturally appropriate way. Two reasons people reject the idea that Jesus claimed to be God:

1. People have an idea of who God is, and Jesus doesn't fit into that idea.
2. People have an idea of who Jesus is, and God doesn't fit into that idea.

Jesus challenges both of those ideas in the New Testament, as he presents and positions himself as Jesus *and* God—Israel's God.

> He claimed divinity in every way that mattered and made sense to the first-century Jewish world.
>
> —MARK CLARK

Jesus offered membership in the renewed people of the covenant God on his own authority and by his own process.

—N. T. WRIGHT

We Need to Rethink Jesus and Our Understanding of God in Light of Jesus

One of Jesus' central claims was to teach the world about God.

The cross wasn't only about salvation from sin; it was a statement about God.

Jesus wept.

—JOHN 11:35

The reason [Jesus] weeps is because he wants to enter in. He wants to enter in to the grief, and the trauma, and the pain of their hearts. He wants to enter in to the human experience.

—TIM KELLER

God Comes alongside Us *in Jesus.*

God entered the human story as:

- a burning bush
- a cloud by day
- fire by night
- in the tabernacle and the temple

Christianity isn't about a temporary experience of God becoming a man. The incarnation isn't just for a time. In a sense, it's for all time.

—MARK CLARK

The human form of Jesus will last for eternity.

God became one of us. Christianity is the only faith making that claim.

Key question: What did Jesus teach us about God?

It was the contention of [the New Testament writers] that with the coming of Jesus the whole situation of mankind has so altered as to change the semantic content of the word "God."

—G. B. CAIRD

Those who have desired to explore and understand the incarnation itself have regularly missed what is arguably the most central, shocking and dramatic source material on that subject, which if taken seriously would ensure that the meaning of the word "god" be again and again rethought around the actual history of Jesus himself.

—N. T. WRIGHT

Jesus was asked, "What are you?!" not just "Who are you?"

He said over and over that he was God.

Jump ahead to the group discussion if you're doing this session in two parts.

NOTES: PART B

——— God Is Known through Jesus ———

Jesus claimed he is *the way to* God, and he is *the person of* God.

THE CLAIMS AND CHALLENGES OF JESUS

- God exists (the challenge to atheism).
- There is only one God (the challenge to Hinduism).
- He is human and divine (the challenge to Judaism and Islam).
- God is knowable (the challenge to agnosticism).

The claims of Jesus are the answers to our deepest longings.

God became one of us to bring us home.

For God so loved the world that he gave his one and only Son, that whoever believes in him shall not perish but have eternal life.

—JOHN 3:16

God was motivated by love.

God gave us love through the person of Jesus.

God becomes one of us to save us.

——— Concepts of God ———

Some of us are overwhelmed by concepts of God as:

- Distant
- Judgmental
- Keeping records of our rights and wrongs

But then Jesus shows up and gives us a different understanding of God in light of who he was:

- Suffering servant
- Others-centered
- Motivated by love

Key question: Will we see Jesus as the one who brings the mystery of God into light for us?

——— Jesus as the Only Way ———

Did Jesus Actually Claim to Be the Only Way?

> Jesus answered, "I am the way and the truth and the life. No one comes to the Father except through me."
>
> —JOHN 14:6

Jesus *is* the way.

> Salvation is found in no one else, for there is no other name under heaven given to mankind by which we must be saved.
>
> —ACTS 4:12

> But small is the gate and narrow the road that leads to life, and only a few find it.
>
> —MATTHEW 7:14

> Lord, are only a few people going to be saved?
>
> —LUKE 13:23

> Strive to enter by the narrow door; for many, I tell you, will seek to enter and will not be able. When once the householder has risen up and shut the door, you will begin to

stand outside and to knock at the door, saying, "Lord, open to us." He will answer you, "I do not know where you come from."

—LUKE 13:24–25 RSV

There will be weeping there, and gnashing of teeth, when you see Abraham, Isaac and Jacob and all the prophets in the kingdom of God, but you yourselves thrown out.

—LUKE 13:28

So Why Do So Few People Find the Way?

We aren't willing to get over the hurdles of our pride and self-sufficiency.

Gnosticism is *an ancient belief in a private, mysterious knowledge or spirituality that was about you as an individual.*

Truth in that kind of mentality, and that ideology was not found in class struggle or political consciousness, but rather in the journey into the self. Politics had been superseded by psychology. The counter cultural revolution had morphed into a therapeutic quest to discover individual fulfillment.

—MARK SAYERS

We can't save ourselves; only God can save us.

The most countercultural act one can commit in [our] culture is to break its only taboo: to commit self-disobedience.

—MARK SAYERS

Jesus and the rest of the Bible are clear on the idea that there is only one person who can save.

The problem of sinfulness is only solved through the cross and resurrection.

KEY QUESTIONS

Jesus is the only way to what?

If there is a heaven, how do we get there?

What does Jesus claim to be the only way to?

My Father's house has many rooms; if that were not so, would I have told you that I am going there to prepare a place for you?

—JOHN 14:2

Jesus makes an exclusive claim about the way to his Father's house.
Jesus says heaven is a resurrected life.

The real treasure of heaven is not the place but the person who's prepared it. God is the greatest reward of all.

—MARK CLARK

The image Jesus uses to communicate the joy of heaven is that of a *homecoming*—a *house*, a *home*, the concept of *arriving*.

The Longing for Home

The longing for home is difficult to satisfy.

It's like a spiritual homesickness, a sense that we were built for something that transcends our human experience. And once in a while, something pokes through our busy lives. And we think, this is what I was built for, this is what I long for more than anything. And then it's gone.

—MARK CLARK

If we find in ourselves a desire that nothing in this world can satisfy, the most probable explanation is that we were made for another world.

—C. S. LEWIS

We were made for *more*—for reality beyond the place we seek.

What Keeps Us from That Reality?

Our sin keeps us from the reality of heaven. This is the problem Jesus came to address.

You have made us for Yourself, and our hearts are restless until they rest in You.

—SAINT AUGUSTINE OF HIPPO

——— Does the Claim by Jesus to Be the Exclusive Way ——— to Salvation Make Rational Sense?

The Law of Noncontradiction: *two opposite ideas about God and salvation can't be true at the same time.*

We can't settle for false realities out of fear.

Christianity is not the only worldview that claims exclusivity. Even those most tolerant views have exclusivity.

——— Christianity as the Only Way to Salvation ———

Our salvation lies not in an escape from this world, but in the transformation of this world. . . . The biblical vision is unique. That is why when someone says that there is salvation in other faiths, I ask them, 'What salvation are you talking about?' No faith holds out a promise of eternal salvation for the world the way the cross and the resurrection of Jesus do.

—VINOTH RAMACHANDRA

Key question: What does salvation mean?

Jesus is the only way to God. The path to salvation in Jesus is to a new heaven and a new earth.

Group Discussion

Take a few minutes to discuss what you just watched and explore these concepts in Scripture.

PART A

1. What stood out to you from Mark's teaching on the problem of Jesus as God?

_____

_____

_____

_____

_____

_____

_____

2. **Read Philippians 2:1–11.** What does this passage tell us about the early church and their perspective of Jesus?

_____

_____

_____

_____

_____

3. **Read John 14:1–4.** How does Jesus comfort his disciples? How does this passage bring comfort to you?

_____

_____

_____

_____

_____

4. What changes about our lives when we choose to trust Jesus as God?

_____

_____

_____

_____

_____

If you're doing session 7 in two parts, pause your discussion here. Take time to pray together as a group. Use the space at the end of this session to keep track of prayer requests and group updates. Otherwise, continue answering the questions for part B of your group discussion.

PART B

5. How do the claims of Jesus challenge other worldviews?

_____

_____

_____

_____

6. What was your concept of God prior to knowing much about Jesus or having a real relationship with him?

    _____

    _____

    _____

7. **Read Matthew 7:7–29.** What warnings and encouragements does Jesus give in this passage? Pick the warning or encouragement that stands out most to you—how does this shape the way you live your everyday life?

    _____

    _____

    _____

8. **Read Hebrews 2.** According to this passage, how did God testify to his salvation through Jesus?

    _____

    _____

    _____

Pray

Pray as a group before you close your time together. Thank God for the ways he has "moved into the neighborhood" and entered the mess of our human lives through the humanity and divinity of Jesus. Ask God for wisdom, grace, and love as you explain the exclusivity of God through Jesus to those who ask about it. Thank God that Jesus made a way for us to be reconciled to God through sacrifice and salvation. Use this space to keep track of prayer requests and group updates.

_____

_____

_____

_____

_____

_____

Between-Sessions
PERSONAL STUDY

Weekly Reflection

Before you begin the between-sessions exercises, briefly review your video notes for session 7. In the space below, write down the *most significant point* you took away from this session.

_____
_____
_____
_____
_____
_____
_____
_____
_____
_____
_____

Take some time to reflect on the material you covered during your group time by engaging in any or all of the following between-sessions exercises. These exercises follow the flow of the group experience with two exercises per each part of this session. As you read and experience the material, you may want to make a few notes in your guide. The primary goal of these between-sessions exercises is for your own spiritual growth and personal reflection, and it is not a requirement for group participation. *Note: the verses to read have most likely appeared in other areas of this session as well, but they are placed in these exercises for intentional reflection.* If you haven't done so already, read chapters 13 and 14 in *The Problem of Jesus*.

Part A

Day 1: Jesus as God in the Early Church
Read: *Philippians 2:1–11; Colossians 1:16–26; 2:9*

Consider: The apostle Paul spoke of Jesus as God in his letters to the Colossians and Philippians. These letters, often dated in the early to mid-50s AD, were most likely written before the Gospels and point to the notion that the first Christians unquestionably spoke about Jesus as God. To a Jew like Paul, creational monotheism was an essential doctrine of God, meaning God was one, he was the Creator, and he shared glory with no one. Yet in passage after passage, Paul ascribed the titles of God and his creational acts and essence to Jesus. For the early Christians, the incarnation was "God plus" (God the Son plus a human nature in Jesus) rather than "God minus" (the loss of deity or divine attributes in the human Jesus). Paul and the rest of the New Testament writers reshape the concept of divinity around Jesus while retaining the earlier commitment to Jewish monotheism in what was coined in theological circles as "Christological monotheism." And this can be seen and heard in the creeds and hymns of the early church. Contrary to skeptical myths, the early church worshiped Jesus as God and came to view him as fully divine and fully human. This was not heresy or an impossibility—it was the reality around which they shaped their lives.

Reflect: Take a few moments to reflect on your answers to these questions.

How does the reality that Paul wrote his early letters prior to the writing of the Gospels shape or change the way you hear Paul's message about Jesus?

_____

_____

_____

_____

_____

How did Paul's Jewish audience respond or react to his teaching?

_____

_____

_____

_____

What changed for the Jews who were now followers of Jesus? How did faith or church life look different for them?

_____

_____

_____

_____

_____

Pray: Close your time today by praying to God. Pray whatever comes to mind as you consider these passages and these questions.

Day 2: Jesus as God in the Gospels
Read: *Review the list of Jesus' claims on pages 224–27 in* The Problem of Jesus.

Consider: When we dig into the Gospels, we see clearly that Jesus made repeated claims to be God, both overtly and subversively, and that his early followers also believed this to be true. But a word of caution for all of us: *not having our own firm experience of the historical Jesus makes understanding him that much harder.* We make the mistake of assuming Jesus would reveal things about himself in the same way *we* would; therefore, we understand him based on our own feelings and agendas. But this is simply not the truth of who he really was. Jesus made his claim to be God through the words and methods first-century Jews would understand. And he did so in a way that ensured his message wouldn't be mistaken for one that was compatible with existing mythical worldviews, such as pantheism. The world Jesus lived and breathed in responded right on cue with what he said and what he did. His claims were confusing at first, but they were not lost on his audience. And the same goes for his actions. For the list of what Jesus said and did, revisit your teaching notes, or turn to pages 224–27 in *The Problem of Jesus*.

Reflect: Take a few moments to reflect on your answers to these questions.

How have you assumed that the words and actions of Jesus meant something that corresponded with your own thoughts, feelings, or agenda, when they actually meant something else in their first-century context?

_____

_____

_____

_____

What can you do to prevent this kind of assumption as you continue to study the words of Jesus in Scripture?

_____

_____

_____

What claims and actions of Jesus stand out to you? How do they make Jesus more real for you?

_____

_____

_____

Pray: Close your time today by praying to God. Pray whatever comes to mind as you consider these passages and these questions.

Part B

Day 3: Jesus as God in Modern Day
Read: *Romans 8:28–38*

Consider: Today we are living in a time when, philosophically, you can believe anything so long as you do not claim it to be true. Morally, you can practice anything so long as you do not claim it is a "better" way. We are fixed in a particular cultural mood—one that seems to crush reason under the weight of feeling. Our feelings are defining reality for us, and the religious paradigms making a modern-day comeback seem to be a hybrid of Western marketing and Eastern mythology. The initial casualties in such a mix are *truth* and *the person of God*. This is why the claim of Jesus—that God not only exists but also is knowable exclusively through Jesus—is so scandalous today. Jesus claimed that he is the way to God and that he is the person of God. He challenges atheism by claiming that God exists. He challenges Hinduism by saying that there is only one God. He challenges Islam and Judaism by claiming that he, a man, is divine. And he challenges agnosticism by saying that God is knowable. No matter what our view is, Jesus won't let us fit him into our way of thinking. He confronts us and won't let us off the hook until we've made a decision about him. In his claims we find the answers to our deepest longings, and we find hope because not only does God exist but he became one of us to bring us home. That is how much God is for us and after us, even still today.

Reflect: Take a few moments to reflect on your answers to these questions.

How have you experienced the modern-day philosophical idea that Jesus is divine as we are all divine? What is your response to this idea?

_____

_____

_____

_____

How has Jesus confronted you with his claim to be God and not let you "off the hook" until you've made a decision about him?

_____

_____

_____

_____

What is it like for you to claim Jesus as God in your life? Is this concept widely accepted, rejected, or challenged in your family, your circle of friends, or your community?

_____

_____

_____

_____

Pray: Close your time today by praying to God. Pray whatever comes to mind as you consider these passages and these questions.

Day 4: The Only Way
Read: *Matthew 7:13–14; Luke 13:23–24; John 14:4–6; Acts 4:12*

Consider: To our modern-day culture that insists all religions and spiritual views are true, the exclusive claim that Jesus is the *only way* to experience salvation sounds judgmental, bigoted, and narrow-minded. That's why this claim is the only thing more scandalous to a modern skeptic than the idea that Jesus is God. But if what we have said so far is true, that Jesus is indeed God, then he must be the only way, because exclusivity is a natural corollary to the fact of Jesus being God. If we take a good look at the Gospels, it is clear that Jesus saw himself as the only way to God and, consequently, to salvation. He addresses it *implicitly* on almost every page of the

Gospels and *specifically* in his recorded conversations at crucial moments like his interaction with Thomas in John 14. Jesus isn't just blazing a trail or giving us the right teaching to point us along the true path—he's saying he *is* the path, the *only* path. No religion, worldview, or behavior can save us, only Jesus can. Salvation is not about what we do for God; it's about what he did for us. In today's world, it's not popular to give up what we want to follow the will of another, but Jesus was clear when he said: "Deny yourself, pick up your cross, and follow me." His followers doubled down on the message by preaching it too. The Bible is clear that Jesus is the only way to heaven, so we can be clear on that too. No other person gives us the ability to be saved because Jesus is the only one who deals with our problems of sin, death, and distance from God. All of these problems are made right through the death and resurrection of Jesus Christ.

Reflect: Take a few moments to reflect on your answers to these questions.

Do you truly believe Jesus is the only way? Why or why not?

_____

_____

_____

_____

What doubts or questions remain for you? Or what doubts or questions do you hear expressed in the world around you—your friends, family, colleagues, or community members?

_____

_____

_____

_____

How does this session on "The Problem of Jesus as God—Or God as Jesus" help you understand and explain the truth the Jesus is the only way to our salvation?

_____

_____

_____

_____

Pray: Close your time today by praying to God. Pray whatever comes to mind as you consider these passages and these questions.

For Next Week: Read chapters 15 and 16 in *The Problem of Jesus* and use the space below to write any insights or questions from your personal study that you want to discuss at the next group meeting.

_____

_____

_____

_____

_____

_____

_____

Journal, Reflections, and Notes

_____

_____

_____

_____

_____

_____

_____

_____

_____

_____

_____

_____

_____

_____

_____

_____

_____

The Problem of
JESUS' DEATH

When the centurion, who stood there in front of Jesus, saw how he died, he said "Surely this man was the Son of God!"

—MARK 15:39

Welcome

Have you ever stopped to think about why we call Good Friday "good"? It's the meaning of Jesus' death that makes it *good*, not the dying itself. Jesus' death was brutal and bloody, but the significance of that death is not only good—it's *great*! There is little doubt from a historical perspective that Jesus' crucifixion happened. His death was recorded and his resurrection alluded to by multiple sources at or shortly after the time of Jesus, including non-Christian and nonbiblical historians. Believers and skeptics alike have had to face the question of Jesus' death and resurrection. If these events truly happened as we believe they did, then they are *the single-most defining event in history*. These events surrounding Jesus' death and resurrection define how God, the Creator of all things, relates with humankind, and they decide the fate of every person who has ever lived. These events, as presented in the Gospels, are the pivot-point from which all of history moves in a different direction from where it was going. And all four Gospels in the New Testament clearly state that Jesus was crucified. There is absolutely no room to question the death of Jesus with the precision of details about the location of the event, the historical markers, and the specific explanations of the judiciary systems and torturous practices of the Roman government. So why do some still question his death? This is the problem of Jesus' death for scholars and skeptics alike. Let's take a closer look together.

Share

To kick things off, briefly discuss one of the following statements:

- Name something in your life that consistently reminds you about the death of Jesus.

  —*or*—

- What image comes to mind when you think about the death of Jesus?

Read

Invite someone to read aloud the following passage as preparation for Mark's teaching. Listen for fresh insights as you hear the verses being read, and then briefly discuss the questions that follow.

Jesus Arrested

Just as he was speaking, Judas, one of the Twelve, appeared. With him was a crowd armed with swords and clubs, sent from the chief priests, the teachers of the law, and the elders.

Now the betrayer had arranged a signal with them: "The one I kiss is the man; arrest him and lead him away under guard." Going at once to Jesus, Judas said, "Rabbi!" and kissed him. The men seized Jesus and arrested him. Then one of those standing near drew his sword and struck the servant of the high priest, cutting off his ear.

"Am I leading a rebellion," said Jesus, "that you have come out with swords and clubs to capture me? Every day I was with you, teaching in the temple courts, and you did not arrest me. But the Scriptures must be fulfilled." Then everyone deserted him and fled.

A young man, wearing nothing but a linen garment, was following Jesus. When they seized him, he fled naked, leaving his garment behind.

They took Jesus to the high priest, and all the chief priests, the elders and the teachers of the law came together. Peter followed him at a distance, right into the courtyard of the high priest. There he sat with the guards and warmed himself at the fire.

The chief priests and the whole Sanhedrin were looking for evidence against Jesus so that they could put him to death, but they did not find any. Many testified falsely against him, but their statements did not agree.

Then some stood up and gave this false testimony against him: "We heard him say, 'I will destroy this temple made with human hands and in three days will build another, not made with hands.'" Yet even then their testimony did not agree.

Then the high priest stood up before them and asked Jesus, "Are you not going to answer? What is this testimony that these men are bringing against you?" But Jesus remained silent and gave no answer.

Again the high priest asked him, "Are you the Messiah, the Son of the Blessed One?"

"I am," said Jesus. "And you will see the Son of Man sitting at the right hand of the Mighty One and coming on the clouds of heaven."

The high priest tore his clothes. "Why do we need any more witnesses?" he asked. "You have heard the blasphemy. What do you think?"

They all condemned him as worthy of death. Then some began to spit at him; they blindfolded him, struck him with their fists, and said, "Prophesy!" And the guards took him and beat him. (Mark 14:43–65)

What is one key insight that stands out to you from this passage?

_____

_____

_____

Why do you think Jesus remains silent against the false accusations and claims others are making about him?

_____

_____

_____

Consider as you listen to Mark's teaching: *What does the death of Jesus mean for us today?*

_____

_____

_____

Watch ▶

Play the video segment for session 8. As you watch, use the following outline to record any thoughts or concepts that stand out to you.

NOTES: PART A

——— The Significance of the Death and Resurrection of Jesus ———

This is the pivot point for all of history.

Key question: What actually took place around the death and resurrection of Jesus?
Key question: What does it mean for us?

——— The Events of Jesus' Death ———

The death of Jesus is documented by historical and extrabiblical sources.

> About this time there lived Jesus, a wise man, if indeed one ought to call him a man, for he wrought surprising feats. He was the Christ. When Pilot condemned him to be crucified, those who had come to love him did not give up their affection for him. On the third day, he appeared restored to life. And the tribe of Christians has not disappeared.
>
> —JOSEPHUS, *ANTIQUITIES* (AD 37)

All four Gospels tell us Jesus was crucified:

- It happened in Jerusalem during the reign of Pilot and Herod.
- There was an earthquake.
- They detail the judicial system and torture practices of the Roman government.

WHY CRUCIFIXION?

- It was a public and a political message because Jesus was considered a rebel leader.
- Jesus was crucified as a revolutionary.
- Jesus was seen as a threat to the empire.
- Jesus was also crucified because of the Jewish charges against him (Mark 14).

> Then the chief priests and the Pharisees called a meeting of the Sanhedrin. "What are we accomplishing?" they asked. "Here is this man performing many signs. If we let him go on like this, everyone will believe in him, and then the Romans will come and take away both our temple and our nation."
>
> —JOHN 11:47–48

Jesus was flogged and then crucified. (Matthew 27)

> Just as there were many who were appalled at him—
>> his appearance was so disfigured beyond that of any human being
>> and his form marred beyond human likeness.
>> —ISAIAH 52:14

Death on a cross would have been *excruciating*.

———— The Meaning of the Cross and Crucifixion ————

The cross is the symbol that has come to represent Christianity.

> Without the cross, the teaching ministry of Jesus is a series of nice ideas about God and life. But it doesn't solve anything. Christianity proclaims that something meaningful happened when Jesus died—something that changes reality and how we relate to God.
>
> —MARK CLARK

———— Foundational Understandings of the Death of Jesus ————

1. The atonement for sin

> Now from the sixth hour there was darkness over all the land until the ninth hour.
> —MATTHEW 27:45 RSV

The Jews would gather daily at the ninth hour to offer sacrifices as atonement for their sin—which makes Jesus the ultimate sacrifice for sin.

> But as it is, he has appeared once for all at the end of the age to put away sin by the sacrifice of himself. And just as it is appointed for men to die once, and after that comes judgment, so Christ, having been offered once to bear the sins of many.
> —HEBREWS 9:26–28 RSV

In his dying, Jesus was not only a witness and a guide, a martyr and a hero, a prophet and a King. He was above all active in it as a priest. It is his high priestly function which in his death comes out into the foreground the most. His dying was the sacrifice freely given to the Father by him.

—HERMAN BAVINCK

2. Jesus as our substitute

For the essence of sin is man substituting himself for God, while the essence of salvation is God substituting himself for man.

—JOHN STOTT

For the Son of man also came not to be served but to serve, and to give his life as a ransom for many.

—MARK 10:45 RSV

Ransom means *substitute*.

Jump ahead to the group discussion if you're doing this session in two parts.

NOTES: PART B

2. Jesus as our substitute (continued)

There are many who preach about the Lord Jesus to no effect and we can see why. They have no doctrine of sin, they never convict or convince people of sin. They always hold Christ before men and say that that is enough. But it is not enough; for the effect of sin upon us is such that we shall never fly to Christ until we realize that we are paupers.

—D. MARTYN LLOYD-JONES

Jesus will never be your hero until you recognize your plight.

—MARK CLARK

Jesus defeated sin. This is what the cross is all about—*atonement*.

As Tim Keller put it, the means of salvation is the cross, and the trajectory of salvation is restoration.

In sinning, our original relationship with God was broken, and there are consequences of that sin, the most profound being *our detachment from true love.*

The serpent harms the person who is destroying him (Genesis 3).

He forgave us all our sins, having canceled the charge of our legal indebtedness, which stood against us and condemned us; he has taken it away, nailing it to the cross. And having disarmed the powers and authorities, he made a public spectacle of them, triumphing over them by the cross.

—COLOSSIANS 2:13–15

At the cross, Satan, sin, and death are being defeated as Jesus is dying.

The fatal wound from the serpent is also the climactic victory for Jesus.

—MARK CLARK

Jesus had to allow evil to do its worst to him in order to put it out of commission.

There are dozens of ways to deal with evil in our lives and several ways to conquer it. All of them are facets of the truth that the only ultimate way to conquer evil is to let it be smothered within a willing, living human being. When it is absorbed there like blood in a sponge or a spear into one's heart, it loses its power and goes no further. . . . Whenever this happens, there is a slight shift in the balance of power in the world.

—M. SCOTT PECK

That's what's happening at the cross.

Jesus takes the Passover feast and makes the meal about him (Luke 22:19–20).

He tells the disciples that this is how they will be free from the slavery of sin and death.

The two symbols of Jesus in the temple and the upper room:

i. *The present system is corrupt, ripe for judgement, but Jesus is Messiah who will save the world.*
ii. *This is how the true exodus will come about, how evil will be defeated, and how sin will be forgiven.*

The good news: Jesus shed his blood for all of us as we are guilty of our own sins. The cross solves our deepest need.

> If God had perceived that our greatest need was economic, he would have sent an econo-mist. If he had perceived that our greatest need was entertainment, he would have sent us a comedian or an artist. If God had perceived that our greatest need was political stability, he would have sent us a politician. If he had perceived that our greatest need was health, he would have sent us a doctor. But he perceived that our greatest need involved our sin, our alienation from him, our profound rebellion, our death; and he sent us a Savior.
>
> —D. A. CARSON

3. The propitiation of Jesus

   The term is used four times in the New Testament:
   - Romans 3
   - Hebrews 2
   - 1 John 2
   - 1 John 4

   It means:
   - A *sacrifice of atonement*
   - A *turning of the wrath of God into favor*

   Propitiation is why the modern world neglects the cross—because of the idea of the wrath of God.

> For I know that good itself does not dwell in me, that is, in my sinful nature. For I have the desire to do what is good, but I cannot carry it out.
>
> —ROMANS 7:18

The need for justice.

> Whoever believes in the Son has eternal life, but whoever rejects the Son will not see life, for God's wrath remains on them.
>
> —JOHN 3:36

The wrath of God is like a tsunami, and we get to hide behind the cross.

Key question: What if I still have doubts?

—— Doubts and Faith in Jesus ——

It's not the strength of your faith but the object that you put that faith in that saves you. It's not the depth and purity of your heart but the work of Jesus on your behalf that saves you.

—MARK CLARK

The deep reality of the cross.

> We all, like sheep, have gone astray,
>   each of us has turned to our own way;
> and the LORD has laid on him
>   the iniquity of us all.

—ISAIAH 53:6

Jesus is our sacrifice because of the cross.

> Jesus could have just climbed down. Actually, he could have just said a word and made it all stop. . . . But Jesus stayed.

—SALLY LLOYD-JONES

Maybe all the miracles of Jesus are a preamble to the cross.
Jesus' death "blots out" our sin.

> I, even I, am he who blots out
>   your transgressions, for my own sake,
>   and remembers your sins no more.

—ISAIAH 43:25

> You will again have compassion on us;
>   you will tread our sins underfoot
>   and hurl all our iniquities into the depths of the sea.

—MICAH 7:19

——— The Gift of Jesus' Death on the Cross ———

This gift is the definition of grace.

> Father, forgive them, for they do not know what they are doing.
> —LUKE 23:34

Key question: What are you going to do with it?

Group Discussion

Take a few minutes to discuss what you just watched and explore these concepts in Scripture.

PART A

1. What stood out to you from Mark's teaching on the problem of Jesus' death?

   _____

   _____

   _____

   _____

   _____

2. **Read Matthew 27:11–56.** This is the full crucifixion story of Jesus. What else do you notice in this story as a result of Mark's teaching?

   _____

   _____

   _____

   _____

   _____

3. What do you say to the skeptic or the unbeliever who wonders why God would allow Jesus to experience such a painful death?

   _____

   _____

   _____

   _____

4. **Read Matthew 28:16–20.** How does the crucifixion and resurrection of Jesus give him the authority he claims here? How does this passage influence or guide the way you live your lives as individuals and as a community?

_____

_____

_____

_____

_____

If you're doing session 8 in two parts, pause your discussion here. Take time to pray together as a group. Use the space at the end of this session to keep track of prayer requests and group updates. Otherwise, continue answering the questions for part B of your group discussion.

PART B

5. What did Mark mean when he said, "Jesus will never be your hero until you recognize your plight"? What plight do you need to recognize or acknowledge in your life?

_____

_____

_____

_____

6. **Read Colossians 2.** According to the apostle Paul, what made us dead, and what makes us alive? What encouragement does Paul give us for how to live in light of the atonement of Christ?

_____

_____

_____

_____

7. What doubts or questions do you have about faith in Jesus or the meaning of Jesus' death? Remember that it's okay to believe *and* have doubts at the same time.

_____

_____

_____

8. **Read Romans 8:1–17.** How is it possible for us to live by the Spirit? And what does it look like to do this today? How do we show up in the world around us differently than before when we live by the Spirit?

_____

_____

_____

_____

Pray

Pray as a group before you close your time together. If you're struggling with doubt today, ask God to meet you in your doubt and unbelief. Ask God to continue to show you the significance of the crucifixion and death of Jesus in your life and in the world at large. Thank God for restoring us and reconciling us back to him through the sacrifice of Jesus on the cross. Use this space to keep track of prayer requests and group updates.

_____

_____

_____

_____

_____

_____

_____

_____

_____

_____

_____

_____

_____

_____

_____

Between-Sessions
PERSONAL STUDY

Weekly Reflection

Before you begin the between-sessions exercises, briefly review your video notes for session 8. In the space below, write down the *most significant point* you took away from this session.

_____

_____

_____

_____

_____

_____

_____

_____

_____

_____

_____

Take some time to reflect on the material you covered during your group time by engaging in any or all of the following between-sessions exercises. These exercises follow the flow of the group experience with two exercises per each part of this session. As you read and experience the material, you may want to make a few notes in your guide. The primary goal of these between-sessions exercises is for your own spiritual growth and personal reflection, and it is not a requirement for group participation. *Note: the verses to read have most likely appeared in other areas of this session as well, but they are placed in these exercises for intentional reflection.* If you haven't done so already, read chapters 15 and 16 in *The Problem of Jesus*.

Part A

Day 1: Jesus as a Threat
Read: *Mark 14:53; John 11:47–48*

Consider: The truth about Jesus is that he was seen as a threat to the Roman empire. And the Jewish charge against Jesus—as best as we can tell—is based on his claim to be Messiah and his temple actions. Ultimately, the chief priests, elders, and scribes landed on the charge of Jesus as a false prophet leading Israel astray. According to these men, Jesus needed to be killed for his theological statements, which were no small crimes in his day. They accused Jesus of replacing the central and most cherished symbols of Judaism with himself. And this was seen as such a threat to the innocent lives of the general Jewish public who were just trying to follow the ways of God. Jesus had to be silenced and killing him was the only way to do it. The verdict had already been decided long before his formal trial. And the chief priests and Pharisees even documented several private reasons the Jews wished to kill Jesus—namely, his signs and the fear that he would gain more followers and attract the attention of Rome. The Jewish leaders of Jesus' day were *afraid*, afraid that Rome would take things away from them because of Jesus and afraid that everyone would believe he was the true Messiah. These men might have felt different had they stopped to consider that Jesus might be telling the truth, but they were too busy working *for* God, so they never saw God when he finally showed up in the human form of Jesus. This is how threats work: they use fear to blind us from the truth.

Reflect: Take a few moments to reflect on your answers to these questions.

Imagine yourself among the chief priests and Pharisees of Jesus' day. What would it have taken for them to see the truth of who Jesus really was?

What kind of threat does Jesus pose today?

How can you push back the fear of others with the love of God?

_____

_____

_____

_____

Pray: Close your time today by praying to God. Pray whatever comes to mind as you consider these passages and these questions.

Day 2: The Symbol of the Cross
Read: *John 19:18–20; Acts 2:22–24; 1 Corinthians 1:17–19*

Consider: Have you ever stopped to consider why the cross is the symbol of Christianity? Like Mark said in his teaching, it could have been a fishing boat to emphasize the teaching ministry of Jesus or a towel to emphasize his humble servitude. But early Christians didn't choose any of these symbols. Instead, they chose a cross to emphasize the center of the Christian message. Christianity proclaimed that something meaningful happened when Jesus died, for without the cross the teaching ministry of Jesus was just a series of nice ideas about God and life. The death of Jesus on the cross changed reality for us; it changed how we relate to God. Jesus' death solved the greatest problem of all—our sin and separation from God—by providing solutions to several different things that all have deep meaning in the history of the church, such as: *defeat over Satan, freedom from slavery of death and sin, forgiveness for us and by us, necessary sacrifice, the gift of righteousness, justification before God, the satisfaction of God's wrath, and a model for how to live a life of surrender.* The symbol of the cross wasn't just the symbol of Jesus' death, it was the symbol of making things right in order to have resurrected life for all. That is the power of the cross.

Reflect: Take a few moments to reflect on your answers to these questions.

What does the symbol of the cross mean to you?

_____

_____

_____

_____

Where do you most often see this symbol? Are there places where you have been surprised to see this symbol?

_____

_____

_____

_____

How does the symbol of the cross make Jesus more real to you?

_____

_____

_____

Pray: Close your time today by praying to God. Pray whatever comes to mind as you consider these passages and these questions.

Part B

Day 3: Jesus as a Substitute
Read: *John 1:28–30, 35–37; Acts 8:32–33; 1 Peter 1:18–20*

Consider: There's a reason Jesus is referred to as a "lamb" in these passages. An unblemished lamb was the sacrifice requirement for Passover, the most important Jewish holiday under the law of the Old Testament. Passover was a celebration in remembrance of God's deliverance of the Israelites from slavery in Egypt. The blood of the sacrificial lamb was a beautiful symbol to the Jews of Christ's atonement on the cross, meaning that the blood of Jesus protected those for whom he died from their own death. There was another important daily sacrifice involving lambs at the temple in Jerusalem. This sacrifice was made for the sins of the people and the lamb represented the perfect sacrifice of Christ on the cross. Jesus was the lamb—the perfect sacrifice made on our behalf. Jesus went to bat for us, taking the heat of condemnation that was justly coming our way so we didn't have to. Jesus came to our world to do a task: *to give his life as a ransom for many.* He came as a substitute sacrifice on our behalf because we were substituting sin for God. We need salvation. We need God substituting himself for us through Jesus. This sums up the reason Jesus had to die as our substitute and the reason we refer to him as the lamb of God.

Reflect: Take a few moments to reflect on your answers to these questions.

Until today, how have you understood Jesus as the "lamb of God"?

_____

_____

_____

What does it mean for Jesus to be a substitute for you?

_____

_____

_____

How does this perspective of Jesus as a substitute change the way you view Jesus?

_____

_____

_____

Pray: Close your time today by praying to God. Pray whatever comes to mind as you consider these passages and these questions.

Day 4: Victory in Jesus
Read: *Genesis 3; 1 Corinthians 15:1–4, 54–56*

Consider: Sin keeps us from connecting with God. Sin is why Jesus paid a price and suffered on the cross. Sin is what Jesus sets us free from in the resurrection. This freedom is the atonement for sin. This freedom is the victory in Jesus, and it's what the cross is all about. Because of Adam and Eve's choice to sin (Genesis 3), the same sin is now ingrained in each one of us. It is what the Bible refers to as "sinful nature" and what psychologists call a "false self." The original relationship with God was broken with the first sin, and we've repeated the pattern and the brokenness ever since. But God never abandoned Adam and Eve, nor has he abandoned us. Instead, God promised Adam and Eve that he would deal with their sin. God promised there would one day be an offspring of the woman (Christ) who would crush the serpent's (Satan's) head, thereby claiming victory over him and defeating his influence over all of creation. And this victory would happen in the context of the serpent biting the victor's heel—harming the very person who would destroy him. The destruction of the serpent would happen not only at the moment the victor was bit but in the act of being bit. Paul later explained that on the surface of

Jesus' death, the rulers and authorities of the world appeared to be killing Jesus; however, Jesus was being killed by an ancient enemy of the human race, *Satan*. As Jesus was dying on the cross, it was Satan, sin, and death that were being defeated. The fatal wound of Jesus' death was also the climactic victory for Jesus.

Reflect: Take a few moments to reflect on your answers to these questions.

What does it mean for Christians to have victory in Jesus?

_____

_____

_____

Where do you need victory in your life over the power of sin and evil?

_____

_____

_____

What do you want Jesus to do for you in his victorious power?

_____

_____

_____

Pray: Close your time today by praying to God. Pray whatever comes to mind as you consider these passages and these questions.

For Next Week: Read chapters 17 and 18 in *The Problem of Jesus* and use the space below to write any insights or questions from your personal study that you want to discuss at the next group meeting.

_____

_____

_____

_____

_____

_____

_____

Journal, Reflections, and Notes

The Problem of
THE RESURRECTION

I am the resurrection and the life.

—JOHN 11:25

Welcome

Everyone loves a great comeback story. It's part of being human, something hardwired into our psyche. We connect to stories of success, and even more so, we connect to the stories of those who achieve success after tasting failure in a raw, emotional, even visceral way. We cheer for the person who rises out of despair as though they are climbing out of hell one inch at a time. And even more than wanting a perfect hero, we want heroes who have come up through pain and defeat to arrive on the other side—those who have the scars to show for their victorious struggle. We desperately want to know how we, too, can struggle through deep pain and come out on the other side better and stronger for it. We connect to this struggle at a soul level because it's the story God has written on our hearts. In creating us, he knew he would one day come and fulfill that longing for drawing victory out of looming defeat and bringing life out of death. This is the story of the resurrection of Jesus.

Share 💬

To kick things off, briefly discuss one of the following statements:

- Name a time when you suffered defeat and had to "rise from the ashes" of your life or your circumstance.

  —*or*—

- What is your favorite "comeback" story? This could be a true story or a fictional one.

Read 📖

Invite someone to read aloud the following passage as preparation for Mark's teaching. Listen for fresh insights as you hear the verses being read, and then briefly discuss the questions that follow.

Jesus Is Risen

On the first day of the week, very early in the morning, the women took the spices they had prepared and went to the tomb. They found the stone rolled away from the tomb, but when they entered, they did not find the body of the Lord Jesus. While they were wondering about this, suddenly two men in clothes that gleamed like lightning stood beside them. In their fright the women bowed down with their faces to the ground, but the men said to them, "Why do you look for the living among the dead? He is not here; he has risen! Remember how he told you, while he was still with you in Galilee: 'The Son of Man must be delivered over to the hands of sinners, be crucified and on the third day be raised again.'" Then they remembered his words.

When they came back from the tomb, they told all these things to the Eleven and to all the others. It was Mary Magdalene, Joanna, Mary the mother of James, and the others with them who told this to the apostles. But they did not believe the women, because their words seemed to them like nonsense. Peter, however, got up and ran to the tomb. Bending over, he saw the strips of linen lying by themselves, and he went away, wondering to himself what had happened.

Now that same day two of them were going to a village called Emmaus, about seven miles from Jerusalem. They were talking with each other about everything that had happened. As they talked and discussed these things with each other, Jesus himself came up and walked along with them; but they were kept from recognizing him.

He asked them, "What are you discussing together as you walk along?"

They stood still, their faces downcast. One of them, named Cleopas, asked him, "Are you the only one visiting Jerusalem who does not know the things that have happened there in these days?"

"What things?" he asked.

"About Jesus of Nazareth," they replied. "He was a prophet, powerful in word and deed before God and all the people. The chief priests and our rulers handed him over to be sentenced to death, and they crucified him; but we had hoped that he was the one who was going to redeem Israel. And what is more, it is the third day since all this took place. In addition, some of our women amazed us. They went to the tomb early this morning but didn't find his body. They came and told us that they had seen a vision of angels, who said he was alive. Then some of our companions went to the tomb and found it just as the women had said, but they did not see Jesus."

He said to them, "How foolish you are, and how slow to believe all that the prophets have spoken! Did not the Messiah have to suffer these things and then enter his glory?" And beginning with Moses and all the Prophets, he explained to them what was said in all the Scriptures concerning himself.

As they approached the village to which they were going, Jesus continued on as if he were going farther. But they urged him strongly, "Stay with us, for it is nearly evening; the day is almost over." So he went in to stay with them.

When he was at the table with them, he took bread, gave thanks, broke it and began to give it to them. Then their eyes were opened and they recognized him, and he disappeared from their sight. They asked each other, "Were not our hearts burning within us while he talked with us on the road and opened the Scriptures to us?"

They got up and returned at once to Jerusalem. There they found the Eleven and those with them, assembled together and saying, "It is true! The Lord has risen and has appeared to Simon." Then the two told what had happened on the way, and how Jesus was recognized by them when he broke the bread. (Luke 24:1–35)

What is one key insight that stands out to you from this passage?

_____

_____

_____

_____

_____

_____

Why do you think Jesus doesn't reveal his identity to the disciples along the road to Emmaus?

_____

_____

_____

_____

Consider as you listen to Mark's teaching: *What does the resurrection of Jesus mean for us today?*

_____

_____

_____

_____

Watch ▶

Play the video segment for session 9. As you watch, use the following outline to record any thoughts or concepts that stand out to you.

NOTES: PART A

——— Everyone Loves a Comeback Story ———

> We connect even more to those stories that achieve success after tasting failure.
>
> —MARK CLARK

We want heroes who have experienced pain and defeat and who have scars to show for us.
But why?
Resurrection is the reversal of death.
But death seems irreversible.

> Studies show that the thing we miss the most about someone once they die is their presence.
>
> —MARK CLARK

——— The Problem of Death and the Promise of Jesus ———

Jesus promises *hope.*
Key question: How do we find the strength to get up in the morning after experiencing loss?
Our faith is not sentimental. It's real.
Christianity is founded on future hope.

> Is everything sad going to come untrue?
>
> —J. R. R. TOLKIEN

The irreversible can be reversed. This is how Christianity can be the most hopeful option of faith, all because of the resurrection of Jesus from the dead.

The Resurrection of Jesus

> Christianity is a statement, which if false, is of no importance, and, if true, of infinite importance. The one thing it cannot be is moderately important.
> —C. S. LEWIS

The scandal of Christianity is the problem of the resurrection.

Christianity is about something that had happened in a historical moment. This is the vulnerability of Christianity.

Other religions are about living in a different way:

- Buddhism and Hinduism are about "other-worldliness."
- Judaism and Islam are about the study and practice of "the law."

Christianity doesn't survive if it's just about Jesus' teachings or his death.

> The resurrection is what makes [Jesus'] whole life mean what it means.
> —MARK CLARK

> If Christ has not been raised, our preaching is useless and so is your faith.
> —1 CORINTHIANS 15:14

The resurrection is the *truth* about Christianity. That's the *good news*.

What Is the Resurrection?

Key questions: Why did people believe this in the first place? And why were they willing to die for it?

Both *liberal* and *conservative* scholars claim there is something legitimate about the resurrection.

BELIEFS OF THE ANCIENT WORLD

- *Paganism:* movement from the flesh world into the spirit world
- *Judaism:* resurrection would be *all* of Israel at the end of time

Neither idea had a place for one individual rising from death in the middle of time.

—MARK CLARK

EVIDENCE FOR THE RESURRECTION

1. Medical and historical evidence of Jesus' death
2. Evidence of the missing body
3. Evidence of the actual appearances of Jesus
4. Evidence of the empty tomb with the grave clothes
5. Evidence of the rise of the early church

According to scholars, this is a "sufficient condition" for the emergence of the belief that Jesus really did rise from the dead.

OBJECTIONS TO THE RESURRECTION

1. Jesus never really died.
2. The body was stolen.

Eyewitnesses to the empty tomb were women.
The rise of the early church baffles historians.

Christianity grew from a group of twelve disciples to over thirty-three million people in just 350 years, and by AD 400 over half of the entire population of the Roman empire was Christian.

—MARK CLARK

Christianity is life-changing and legitimate.
Jump ahead to the group discussion if you're doing this session in two parts.

NOTES: PART B

——— **What the Resurrection Has to Do with Us** ———

Celebration and Skepticism (John 20)
Mary's response:

"They have taken my Lord away," she said, "and I don't know where they have put him."
—JOHN 20:13

Thomas' response:

But he said to them, "Unless I see the nail marks in his hands and put my finger where the nails were, and put my hand into his side, I will not believe."
—JOHN 20:25

It's not until they both *see* Jesus that they believe.
Jesus knows skeptics need proof.

Then Jesus told him, "Because you have seen me, you have believed; blessed are those who have not seen and yet have believed."
—JOHN 20:29

Key question: Will we believe?

By this gospel you are saved, if you hold firmly to the word I preached to you. Otherwise, you have believed in vain. For what I received I passed on to you as of first importance: that Christ died for our sins according to the Scriptures, that he was buried, that he was raised on the third day according to the Scriptures.
—1 CORINTHIANS 15:2–4

He was delivered over to death for our sins and was raised to life for our justification.
—ROMANS 4:25

. . . having been buried with him in baptism, in which you were also raised with him through your faith in the working of God, who raised him from the dead.
—COLOSSIANS 2:12

——— The Benefits of Christianity ———

The gateway to these benefits is the resurrection.

And if the Spirit of him who raised Jesus from the dead is living in you, he who raised Christ from the dead will also give life to your mortal bodies because of his Spirit who lives in you.

—ROMANS 8:11

We will all experience resurrection someday.
Resurrection unto *judgement*.

"Do not be amazed at this, for a time is coming when all who are in their graves will hear his voice and come out—those who have done what is good will rise to live, and those who have done what is evil will rise to be condemned."

—JOHN 5:28–29

Resurrection unto *life*.
A new creation: a new heaven and new earth (Revelation 21–22)
We will live in a resurrected, glorified state for all of eternity.
What we do with our lives and what we believe about the resurrection of Jesus actually matters (1 Corinthians 15).

—— The Hope of Christianity ——

I am the resurrection and the life. The one who believes in me will live, even though they die; and whoever lives by believing in me will never die.

—JOHN 11:25

We actually have the gift of living *two* lives when we trust in Jesus.

. . . the life after life after death.

—N. T. WRIGHT

Some day you will read in the papers that D. L. Moody, of East Northfield, is dead. Don't you believe a word of it! At that moment I shall be more alive than I am now.

—D. L. MOODY

The miracle of the Resurrection, and the theology of that miracle, comes first: the biography comes later as a comment on it. . . . The 'Resurrection' to which they bore witness was, in fact, not the action of rising from the dead but the state of having risen.

—C. S. LEWIS

The resurrection was an event, and it is who Jesus is now.

Living in a New Way

Resurrection changes everything for everyone, including us.

Religion crushed Jesus so it didn't have to crush us.

—MARK CLARK

Resurrection is the hope of Christianity.

Key question: Do you believe and live in light of the new way of the resurrection?

Group Discussion

Take a few minutes to discuss what you just watched and explore these concepts in Scripture.

PART A

1. What stood out to you from Mark's teaching on the problem of Jesus' resurrection?

   _____

   _____

   _____

   _____

2. **Read 1 Corinthians 15:12–19.** Have you ever questioned or doubted the resurrection of Jesus? What does Paul say here about our faith if the resurrection is untrue?

   _____

   _____

   _____

   _____

3. **Read Luke 24:36–53.** How do the disciples respond to the appearance of Jesus? How would you have responded if you were in the room?

_____

_____

_____

_____

4. **Read John 21.** Why was this appearance of Jesus so significant to the disciples? And what do you notice about the way Jesus interacts with Peter? Why is this significant too?

_____

_____

_____

_____

If you're doing session 9 in two parts, pause your discussion here. Take time to pray together as a group. Use the space at the end of this session to keep track of prayer requests and group updates. Otherwise, continue answering the questions for part 2 of your group discussion.

PART B

5. **Read John 11:25–27.** What is so scandalous about the words Jesus says to Martha and her response to him?

_____

_____

_____

_____

6. **Read John 20:24–29.** Notice how Jesus appears to Thomas *after* the text tells us he appeared to the disciples. What does the sequence of this appearance tell us about Jesus and Thomas?

_____

_____

_____

_____

7. **Read 2 Corinthians 5.** According to this passage, what is the purpose of the Resurrection as it relates to us? How are we to live as a "new creation" while we wait for the future "new creation"?

_____

_____

_____

8. Take an honest assessment of your life. Do you live as though the power of the resurrection is real in you? If not, what changes do you need to make to live this way, and how can this group support you?

_____

_____

_____

_____

Pray

Pray as a group before you close your time together. Thank God for the gift and the power of the resurrection, now living in you. Ask God to continue to show you what the resurrection means for you in your personal and communal relationship with Jesus. Thank God for making all of us a new creation with the resurrection of Jesus. Use this space to keep track of prayer requests and group updates.

_____

_____

_____

_____

_____

_____

_____

_____

_____

Between-Sessions
PERSONAL STUDY

Weekly Reflection

Before you begin the between-sessions exercises, briefly review your video notes for session 9. In the space below, write down the *most significant point* you took away from this session.

_____

_____

_____

_____

_____

_____

_____

_____

_____

_____

_____

_____

_____

Take some time to reflect on the material you covered during your group time by engaging in any or all of the following between-sessions exercises. These exercises follow the flow of the group experience with two exercises per each part of this session. As you read and experience the material, you may want to make a few notes in your guide. The primary goal of these between-sessions exercises is for your own spiritual growth and personal reflection, and it is not a requirement for group participation. *Note: the verses to read have most likely appeared in other areas of this session as well, but they are placed in these exercises for intentional reflection.* If you haven't done so already, read chapters 17 and 18 in *The Problem of Jesus.*

Part A

Day 1: The Hope of the Resurrection
Read: *Isaiah 42:1–4; Acts 2:25–27; 23:5–7*

Consider: More than any other religion or worldview, Christianity is founded on hope. We believe this life—and death—is not the end. This is why it's easier for those who believe Christianity is true to suffer the death or loss of a loved one and still find strength to get up in the morning. This is because our Christian faith has something amazing to say about the finality and hopelessness of death. In the face of all of the problems raised by the person of Jesus as the Son of God, the problem of death and the promise of Jesus may be the most important because of what Jesus offers us in the end: *eternal hope*. A deep hope that gives us life and reverses the tragedy of death in the most beautiful way. Our stories of loss and death are endless—almost too much for the heart to bear. And yet God understands this loss personally and intimately in the loss of his own son, Jesus. The death of Jesus causes us to embrace his suffering, and consequently our own suffering, in deep, meaningful, and hope-filled ways. If we can understand the suffering of Jesus in this way, then we can trust the legitimate work of Jesus as it relates to loss, death, and the future hope of our resurrection in Christ. Resurrection tells us that the irreversible can be reversed. The resurrection of Jesus is what makes Christianity not only true but also the most hopeful option in the marketplace of faith and ideas.

Reflect: Take a few moments to reflect on your answers to these questions.

How does thinking about the resurrection of Jesus make you feel? Jot down the words or phrases that immediately come to mind.

_____

_____

_____

_____

How does the resurrection of Jesus give you hope amid struggle, loss, or sorrow?

_____

_____

_____

_____

Where do you need the hope of Jesus the most in your life right now?

_____

_____

_____

Pray: Close your time today by praying to God. Pray whatever comes to mind as you consider these passages and these questions.

Day 2: The Reality of the Resurrection
Read: *Luke 24; John 20:11–18*

Consider: Skeptics ask why Christianity became a movement if the founder was killed after just three years of teaching. There must have been something more than the teachings of Jesus and his invitation to live a good, moral life to cause an entire new movement of faith that has lasted for thousands of years. Something must have grabbed ahold of these first-century followers to convince them that Jesus was worth the risk. And this something couldn't have been his death alone because others have died after making the same messianic claims without inciting the same world-changing movement. In fact, Rome killed those they saw as "revolutionaries"—other Jewish teachers who claimed to be the Messiah for a hundred years on either side of the life of Jesus. In some cases, those movements died, and in other cases, someone else, such as a family member, took the supposed Messiah's place. But no one else ever claimed that their leader was now alive again, let alone that he had appeared to his followers, and continued to teach and urge his followers to carry on his mission in his name. Now, it wasn't uncommon for people to claim to see dead people. But this was the first time for claims of someone who died to appear again in real flesh and blood. This is why Christianity is such a scandal—because of the reality of the resurrection. And yet many scholars agree that the resurrection claims of the early church, while unprecedented, are legitimate.

Reflect: Take a few moments to reflect on your answers to these questions.

Imagine being the very people who first experienced the resurrected Christ. What do you think they were thinking and feeling in the moment of realizing it was Jesus?

_____

_____

How do you think you would have responded in the moment?

_____

_____

_____

How does putting yourself in the shoes of the early followers of Jesus make the resurrection more real to you?

_____

_____

_____

Pray: Close your time today by praying to God. Pray whatever comes to mind as you consider these passages and these questions.

Part B

> **Day 3:** Stacking Up the Evidence
> **Read:** *John 20:1–10; 1 Corinthians 15:1–5*

Consider: The evidence for the resurrection of Jesus stacks up in five different categories: *medical and historical evidence, the evidence of a missing body, the evidence of appearances, the evidence of an empty tomb, and the evidence of the rise of the early church.* Given who Jesus was and how good the Romans were at killing, we should accept the medical and historical probability that Jesus really did die and that he wasn't "swooning" in and out of consciousness, waking up later. This just doesn't make sense considering who Jesus was and the way he showed up. Also, a dead body should have been easy to find, and Rome would have wanted to find it too. Then hundreds of people claimed to have seen the resurrected Jesus after his death. Followed by the fact that there were actual grave clothes in the empty tomb. And then the subsequent growth of the Christian movement was historically unprecedented in its speed and fervor. None of these points of evidence prove anything by themselves, nor are they sufficient in arguing for the resurrection on their own. Yet together they make quite the stack of evidence. These pieces of evidence provide "a sufficient condition" for the emergence of the early Christian belief that Jesus really did rise from the dead. What historians find is that this fascinating, crazy claim of the resurrection of Jesus fits exactly where the evidence of history leads.

Reflect: Take a few moments to reflect on your answers to these questions.

What stands out to you about the evidence of the resurrection of Jesus?

_____

_____

_____

Is there something that still doesn't make sense to you? If so, what and why?

_____

_____

_____

The evidence of the resurrection of Jesus infers the best explanation through deductive reasoning that it's actually true. Why then, from your perspective, do people still doubt it?

_____

_____

_____

Pray: Close your time today by praying to God. Pray whatever comes to mind as you consider these passages and these questions.

Day 4: You Only Live Twice
Read: *John 5:28–29; 14:2–3; 20:11–18; Revelation 21–22*

Consider: Our lives today and everything we do with them will echo in eternity. If we ignore the reality that Jesus rose from death and fail to embrace the promised hope God offers, we remain on a trajectory set in motion by the first human sin. Our lives will be cut off from the future purposes of God, serving as a reminder of his justice. Those who remain in their sin will be engulfed by emotional and spiritual pain. And if you trust what Jesus has done and shape your whole life around it, everything good you have done and are doing will be invested in what the Bible calls a "new heaven and a new earth." You will live in a resurrected, glorified state for all eternity. Another way to explain this is to say that we will experience the resurrection of Jesus in one of two ways: either as eternal life or eternal judgement. The latter—eternal judgement—is for those who do not trust in Jesus for salvation. Those who fall into the latter will be bodily raised to live the rest of eternity in the context of spiritual death, wholly distant from goodness, pleasure, God, love, and grace. And the resurrection of eternal life is bodily life in the presence of God and God's new creation: a life of love, grace, peace, delight, community, and pleasures forevermore. But we get to choose. Life beyond death and our own resurrection is the vision our hearts long for—a life beyond sickness and pain and sadness. Our lives now are not the end. And if you trust in Jesus, not even death is the end. The great hope of the Bible is that those who believe in Jesus live on into eternity. But there's one more thought to consider: the idea that we get to live out the resurrected life of Jesus each and every day *before* we face eternity. The resurrection was about Jesus, yes, and about God, yes, and about how he was reconciling the world to himself, yes, but it is also about us. It is about you walking and living in a new way, right now. You get to live your life twice starting today if you trust in the hope of the resurrection.

Reflect: Take a few moments to reflect on your answers to these questions.

What does it stir in you to realize that you have the opportunity to live twice, starting today, because of the resurrection?

_____

_____

_____

_____

Where are you today? Are you headed toward eternal life with God or eternal judgement without God?

_____

_____

_____

What will you do to ensure that you are on the path to eternal life with God? And how will you live your life accordingly in the present?

_____

_____

_____

Pray: Close your time today by praying to God. Pray whatever comes to mind as you consider these passages and these questions.

Journal, Reflections, and Notes

Closing Words

Thank you for joining me for *The Problem of Jesus*. It has been a joy to walk alongside each one of you on your quest for clarity regarding Jesus. My hope is that you now understand why Jesus was such a scandal in the ancient world and what that scandal has to do with our lives today. I pray that you feel challenged and confronted by the problems of Jesus and that this study helped you find comfort in a world that doesn't offer much of that. In our out-of-control world, we can find our place in the teachings, life, death, and resurrection of Jesus in a way that it transforms our lives above the chaos and the noise of our modern day. And we can find the love of Jesus too—something we need now more than ever.

Because of Jesus, we no longer need to feel weighed down under the burden of religion. We don't need to keep setting the fires so the gods will relent, or set out on a pilgrimage so we can earn our way. Jesus fell and stumbled with a cross on his back for us. Religion crushed him so it wouldn't have to crush us. The fury of death, sin, and evil was directed toward him on the cross, and God's anger was satisfied. Jesus made the trek down a dusty road with a beam on his back in our place.

And then the resurrected Jesus left us the greatest gift ever given as he took his position on God's throne: the Spirit of God. The Holy Spirit is also how the acts of Jesus continued throughout the early church—as they do through us today—demonstrating that though Jesus left our world, he is still present and active in our lives until he returns. This means that Christianity is not a story of lives being unmade; *it's about lives being remade*. Our lives mean something—that we can be free, that we can bury our sin with Christ, that we can live on the other side of death and powerlessness, and that we can revel in God's glory. You see, the problems of Jesus have everything to do with us. And because of that reality, there is a new way to be human. This is the hope and the adventure of Christianity.

MARK CLARK

Index of Verses Used
(BY SESSION)

SESSION 1	SESSION 2	SESSION 3	SESSION 4
Opening Verse Luke 4:43	**Opening Verse** John 10:10	**Opening Verse** Matthew 16:24	**Opening Verse** Mark 12:30
Read John 15:1–17	**Read** Mark 8:22–38	**Read** Matthew 19:16–30	**Read** 1 Corinthians 16
Video 1 Corinthians 1:23 Matthew 13:57 Mark 15:21 Mark 10:46 Luke 22:42 1 Corinthians 15:6 Mark 1:15 Luke 4:43 Luke 11:20	**Video** John 5:39–44 John 3:16 John 2 Mark 14:51 Luke 1:1–3a John 5:39–40 John 10:10b John 5:44	**Video** Mark 8:34–35 Matthew 4:6 Matthew 4:3 Matthew 4:9 Matthew 28:18 Hebrews 12:2b-3 Romans 8:18 Matthew 9:36 Mark 10:17–31 Mark 8:35 Luke 9:24 Matthew 28:19–20 John 6:66 Mark 10:36–40	**Video** Mark 12:28 Mark 12:29–31 Romans 1:21 Luke 9:58 Ephesians 4:30 Luke 9:60 Luke 9:62 Psalm 34:8 Psalm 37:4 1 Peter 3:18 Psalm 42:1 John 1:12 John 3:19 1 Corinthians 16:22
Group Discussion Mark 1:9–13 Matthew 9:18–38 Mark 5:21–38 Matthew 2:1–15 Luke 4:42–44	**Group Discussion** John 5:31–47 Matthew 5:1–12 Luke 1:1–4 Luke 3 Matthew 28 Mark 16 Luke 24:1–49 John 20	**Group Discussion** Matthew 4:1–11 Romans 8:12–28 Luke 19:1–10 Galatians 2:14–21 John 6:60–69	**Group Discussion** Matthew 22:34–40 Mark 12:28–34 Genesis 22 1 Samuel 3 Psalm 34 Psalm 37:1–28 1 Corinthians 13
Personal Study *Matthew 28:22–37, Mark 1:1–15, Mark 4:10–12* *Isaiah 35:5–6, Isaiah 53:1–6, Matthew 11:5* *Mark 2:1–12, Luke 7:36–50, Luke 15:11–32* *Mark 1:14–15, Ephesians 2:8–10, Matthew 28:18–20, Romans 7*	**Personal Study** *Matthew 1:1–14, Matthew 5–7, Matthew 28:16–20* *Isaiah 40:1–11, Mark 1:1–8* *Mark 4:10–13* *Luke 1* *1 Samuel 1–2* *John 1:1–18* *John 2:25–59, Exodus 16*	**Personal Study** *Matthew 4:1–11, Luke 9:21–27* *Matthew 16:21–28, Luke 23:26–27, Colossians 1:24–27* *Mark 8:34–38, Matthew 10:37–42, James 2:14–26* *Matthew 28:18–20, Hebrews 12:2, Romans 8:18*	**Personal Study** *Mark 12:28–34* *Matthew 22:36–38, Deuteronomy 6:1–9* *Genesis 3, Luke 9:57–62* *2 Timothy 1:6–12, Ephesians 3:14–21*

185

SESSION 5	SESSION 6	SESSION 7	SESSION 8
Opening Verse John 1:30	**Opening Verse** Luke 15:20	**Opening Verse** John 1:14	**Opening Verse** Mark 15:39
Read Mark 6:30–44	**Read** Luke 15:11–32	**Read** John 1:1–18	**Read** Mark 14:43–65
Video Ephesians 1:19–20 Acts 2:24 John 1:30 John 9:1–2 John 9:39–41 John 2:23 John 20:8 Matthew 12:39 Hebrews 2:3b-4 John 2:6 John 2:18–21 John 2:10 Romans 8:29 Galatians 5:22–23 John 2:4 Luke 22:42 Matthew 10:29 Mark 1:12 Luke 10:23	**Video** Luke 15 John 8:7 John 8:10–11	**Video** John 1:14 The MSG John 1:14 RSV Colossians 1:19 Colossians 2:9 Philippians 2:6 Hebrews 1:2–3 Philippians 2:5–11 Matthew 8:27 John 11:35 John 3:16 John 14:6 Acts 4:12 Matthew 7:14 Luke 13:23 Luke 13:24–25 Luke 13:28 John 14:2	**Video** John 11:47–48 Isaiah 52:14 Matthew 27:45 Hebrews 9:26b-28a Mark 10:45 Colossians 2:13–15 Luke 22:19 Luke 22:20 Romans 7:18 John 3:36 Isaiah 53:6 Isaiah 43:25 Micah 7:19 Luke 23:34
Group Discussion Ephesians 1 Acts 2 Mark 1:16–45 John 2 John 4:43–54 John 20	**Group Discussion** Matthew 13:10–17 Matthew 13 John 8 Luke 15	**Group Discussion** Philippians 2:1–11 John 14:1–14 Matthew 7:7–29 Hebrews 2	**Group Discussion** Matthew 27:11–56 Matthew 28:16–20 Colossians 2 Romans 8:1–17
Personal Study *Luke 21:14–19, Nehemiah 9:16–17, Psalm 77:13–15, Matthew 13:58 Psalm 145:4–6, Romans 1:19–21, Romans 11:23–25 Matthew 8:1–4, Matthew 12:14, Mark 1:40–44 Mark 3:6 John 2:23–25, John 20:8, 29:31, Hebrews 2:3–4*	**Personal Study** *Matthew 13:9–11, Matthew 21:44–26, Mark 4:10–12 Proverbs 1:5–7, Hosea 12:9–10, Matthew 13:34–36 Psalm 25:4–6, Matthew 22:15–22, John 1:16–18 Luke 15*	**Personal Study** *Colossians 1:16–26 and 2:9, Philippians 2:1–11 John 14:4–6, Romans 8:28–38 Matthew 7:13–14, Luke 13:23–24, Acts 4:12*	**Personal Study** *Mark 14:53, John 11:47–48 John 19:18–20, Acts 2:22–24, 1 Corinthians 1:17–19 John 1:28–30 and 35–37, Acts 8:32–33, 1 Peter 1:18–20 Genesis 3, 1 Corinthians 15:1–4 and 54–56*

SESSION 9			
Opening Verse John 11:25			
Read Luke 24:1–35			
Video 1 Corinthians 15:14 John 20:13 John 20:25 John 20:29 1 Corinthians 15:2–4 Romans 4:25 Colossians 2:12 Romans 8:11 John 5:28–29 John 11:25			
Group Discussion 1 Corinthians 15:12–19 Luke 24:36–53 John 21 John 11:25–27 2 Corinthians 5			
Personal Study *Isaiah 42:1–4, Acts 2:25–27, Acts 23:5–7* *Luke 24, John 20:11–18* *John 20:1–10, 1 Corinthians 15:1–5* *John 5:28–29, John 14:2–3* *John 20:11–18, Revelation 21 and 22*			

Leading This Group

Group Size

The Problem of Jesus video study is designed to be experienced in a group setting such as a Bible study, Sunday school class, or any small group gathering. To ensure everyone has enough time to participate in discussions, it is recommended that large groups break up into smaller groups of four to six people each.

Materials Needed

Each participant should have his or her own study guide, which includes notes for video segments, directions for activities, and discussion questions, as well as personal studies to deepen learning between sessions.

Timing

Each session is divided into two parts (A and B) and will take between two and three hours. For those who have less time available to meet, you can use fewer questions for discussion. You may also opt to devote two meetings to each session, covering one of the two parts of each session per meeting.

Facilitation

Each group should appoint a facilitator who is responsible for starting the video and for keeping track of time during discussions and activities. Facilitators may also read questions aloud and monitor discussions, prompting participants to respond and assuring that everyone has the opportunity to participate.

Personal Studies

Maximize the impact of the curriculum with additional study between group sessions. There are four days of personal study available for each session. Feel free to engage with these optional study materials as much or as little as you need.